FURTHER ACCLAIM FOR
THE TECHNOLOGY IMPERATIVE

"(This book) deals with the big challenges of our times, including adapting to destructive technological changes, globalization, massive budget deficits, falling educational attainment, and dysfunction of democracy. It is a clarion call to action while we still have time to set the ship upright".

—**H. Nejat Seyhun, Ph.D,** Professor of Finance and
Jerome B. and Eilene M. York
Professor of Business Administration,
Stephen M. Ross School of Business, University of Michigan.

"THE TECHNOLOGY IMPERATIVE formulates and explores the *paradox of progress* in an engaging, readable, forward-looking manner. This important book serves as both a measure of our technology's success, and the consequent loss in human value. As Psarouthakis's book makes clear, finding economic answers to this paradox in this century is not merely a matter of esthetics and philosophy, but a matter of survival."

—**Theodore Scaltas,**
Professor of Ancient Philosophy,
University of Edinburgh

"This short book is an excellent tool to unlock our minds from the preconceptions of dead-end politics, and a blueprint for shaping the future of a leading, successful, free market nation."

—**Periklis Gogas**, Assistant Professor of Economic Analysis
and International Economics, University of Thrace, Greece

*This book
is dedicated
to all who
honestly seek
a renewable,
sustainable
economy.*

THE
TECHNOLOGY
IMPERATIVE

What 'JOBS! JOBS! JOBS!'
Really Means in the 21st Century

JOHN PSAROUTHAKIS, PH.D

Gavdos Press
Ann Arbor

Cover and interior design by Jacinta Calcut, www.image-gd.com

Published by Gavdos Press, Ann Arbor

ISBN 978-0-9859585-2-7 (perfect bound)
ISBN 978-0-9859585-1-0 (hard cover)

Library of Congress Control Number 2012945165

1 2 3 4 5 16 15 14 13 12

Printed in the United States of America

CONTENTS

Books by
John Psarouthakis, Ph.D

Better Makes Us Best

Managing the Growing Firm

Dynamic Management of Growing Firms
(with Lorraine M. Uhlaner)

Balancing in the Balkans
(with Raymond Tanter)

Elisabeth's Gift

How to Acquire The Right Business
(with Lorraine M. Uhlaner)

The Technology Imperative:
What "Jobs! Jobs! Jobs!"
Really Means in the 21st Century

PREFACE

Six months ago my editor and I sat over coffee discussing several possible book projects. I kept circling back to the one, now completed, that you hold in your hand. If pressed for a working title that day, I might have tried to jam in as much content as possible to describe the concept—something like *Technology, Unemployment, Globalization and What America* Must *Do to Regain Prosperity, Bring Its Economy Back to Life, and Survive in the New Century*. That mouthful sums up the plot (if a non-fiction commentary can be described as having a plot) I had in mind. Every time I began to explain it I became distracted by the subplot That is, these "*must do*" priorities for confronting and conquering an impending national crisis have failed to capture the public imagination despite dire consequences if we fail. Our politicians seem not to understand what is happening. Some ignore the clear facts, while others bark and circle like sheep dogs herding the populace toward the worst possible outcome. The daily mainstream news report has done little to help. I thought I was conveying frustration as I discussed these things, but my editor saw more and offered his own temporary and much shorter working title. "For the moment," he said, "I am going to call this your 'Angry Book'."

My very long career bridging several disciplines included many successes along with the usual number of learning experiences. None of the successes resulted from using anger as a communications tool. Neither resentment nor rage ever solved a physics problem or closed a good business deal. I don't wish to see this book hijacked by my own anger. My editor, however, was spot-on. I *am* angry about what has happened to this country, especially in recent decades, since I arrived here many years ago. I am angry about our continuing descent into dysfunctional government, and—to make it worse—*more* government. Our definitive 21st Century challenge is apolitical, but it is being politicized—to the extent of disparaging and eroding the free-market system that brought us the very prosperity we seek to preserve. My goal here is to point out, directly and forcefully, a challenge we *must* meet and conquer…to define, in the face of widespread misunderstanding, the fundamental nature of that challenge…and to do whatever I can to help generate a sorely needed national conversation.

Our society—our people and our government and our economy—must grasp these issues and respond if we are to sustain, in this century, anything resembling America's achievements and well-being in the previous century. Outlining the very steep risk / reward potentials of the new era yields a list of the very arenas in which I've pursued my life and career—science, technology, business conducted across geopolitical borders, post-smokestack manufacturing, educational reform. It didn't take me long to think: "If a good book idea means a good match of author and subject matter, here we go! Let's write the first page!" Not that I am the only person with this background and these interests; but public discourse these days suggests that every voice pointing out the true impact of technology on our society is a voice that needs to speak up. Besides, I have one substantial new idea to offer in the problem-*solving* department. And in the end I hope to provoke thought about an inevitable future society that will be so different from the 20th Century as to resemble a "Star Trek" destination. The key word is "inevitable." I believe younger readers will live in that futuristic society, or very nearby.

I have harbored, for many years, serious apprehension and

unease about the United States being so very, very slow in addressing public and private policy initiatives demanded by new technology and a global economy. Like many—probably including you—I have long realized how few visionaries we have been sending to Washington as members of elected or bureaucratic institutions, and how these institutions meanwhile have come to demonstrate less and less vision than the sum of their parts. I knew the issues I wished to write about had failed to gain meaningful traction among policymakers and legislators and mass media. I knew trying to help make these issues resonate was important, because the American economy must prove its mettle in brand-new ways or we will sink beneath this new century's history rather than lead and prosper. I understood that we must board this bus *now*, if not sooner. But it was mere urgency, not anger, fueling my desire to write a little book drawing from what I learned in my life and career to help move the process off square one. The anger came when I began thinking about how to frame the message. That's when I fully appreciated the stifling role played by something most of us were already angry about. Let's call it "old business."

Washington has steadfastly refused to deal with three massive pieces of old business: its indebtedness, its monumental pile of unfunded promises via entitlement programs, and its occasionally amusing but mostly tragic and crippling ideological gridlock. Each of those items enormously impacts every American. Together these items add up to a climate in which *nothing* important will be done—nothing *can* be done—about our pressing 21st Century needs. Those needs, meanwhile, must be quickly and effectively addressed or the United States to which we have become accustomed is doomed. That is one grim equation. It is enough to make me—and I assume you—wake up not merely frustrated but white-hot angry. Those of us who are trying to look forward simply cannot do so. Washington must get out of the 20th Century before it can enter the 21st Century, and none of us can get there until Washington gets there. Writing even a chapter about politics and politicians was the very *last* thing on my mind when I first conceived writing about the impact of technology and economic globalization on all of America's tomorrows. But our inability to get from here to there requires discussion, and we'll begin there—anger and all.

I did not, of course, need to write this book to realize the United States has a debt crisis. Nor did I learn only recently that Washington is the only place on earth where unsustainable promises can be propped up for generations by nothing more than hot air and crossed fingers. Nor has it taken me years to recognize ideological warfare masquerading as representative government. Epiphanies, however, can spring from the familiar and the obvious. I hold an engineering degree from MIT, for example, but if I were to drive a motorcycle 100 m.p.h. six inches from the Grand Canyon's rim, then my appreciation of speed and height and several fundamental laws of physics would be greatly enhanced. Similarly, being eager to weigh in with a few observations on vital 21st Century issues, but coming face to face with the fact that no such observations matter until Washington takes care of old business from the 20th Century, strikes me as a compelling insight.

It is indescribably frustrating to realize we face so much peril because of ideological intransigence. The leaders of our representative democracy have the power to turn a hopeless situation into something merely difficult. That's only fair, as they are the ones who made it hopeless in the first place.

— John Psarouthakis
July 2012

CHAPTER ONE

Part of the problem
and part of the solution

A s measured by the calendar, America entered a new century and a new millennium little more than a decade ago.
Delineating a new epoch is not that easy. The next few decades will reveal true, and perhaps game-changing, measure-
ments of where the United States stands. The benchmarks
will be our global status as a developer of new technology, as
a smart manufacturer of value-added products, as an education reformer amid new workplace realities, and as a competitor in the global marketplace. Those are the four vectors of
our national future—"vector" being a better term than benchmark because a vector signals dynamic movement rather than
a mere static measurement. These four vectors—in technology, manufacturing, education, and globalization—will play
recurring roles in this narrative. They will determine whether
we enjoy further generations as a prosperous world leader,
or something less but close to that, or something you would
rather not think about—something your children and grand-
children definitely would rather not think about.

This truly is a new epoch, or era, or age (take your pick)
that we have entered, or are entering, or are about to enter.
Aldous Huxley, in *Brave New World*, drew the American Century's entry point not at the year 1900 but at Henry Ford's
first assembly line. I don't know exactly where historians and

novelists and philosophers will draw our new high-tech journey's embarkation point, and whether it will be as starkly definitive as old Henry's delivery of durable goods and mobility
to the masses.

I do know that the new world now upon us is even more
amazing, but that as someone said in show business, we "ain't
seen nothin' yet." I know technology has been the driving
force of change, as is almost always the case—from the discovery of fire to the personal computer. I know America's
standing as a technological innovator has kept us in the game
as this new era begins, but technology alone cannot keep us
there, and innovation is itself vulnerable to rapid decline. In
other words, of all the "tipping points" one hears about, this is
the big one: Will the United States prevail in this new age, or
will it merely endure? And if it merely endures, how *well* will
it endure? And, by the way, might we be in danger of not even
enduring, at least not in any prosperous way we have come to
expect? Most importantly, what proactive steps must we take
to give ourselves hope for sustaining a competitive edge, perhaps enough to forge another American Century?

That challenge is what THE TECHNOLOGY IMPERATIVE—
this book and our nation's future—is about. First, however,
I need to offer some thoughts about policy and politics, because all the above questions—and all the answers, mine and
yours and anyone else's—will be irrelevant unless and until
the problems discussed in this chapter are defined, addressed,
and solved. If you find that prospect daunting, consider this:
The one institution that must solve these problems is itself the
biggest problem that must be solved. Our intransigent, dysfunctional, gridlocked, elected federal government must ride
to the rescue of itself. It is as if your town council met once a
week discussing old business in perpetuity without acting on

it, meanwhile ignoring vital new agenda items. Tip O'Neill, one of the 20th Century's consummate politicians, famously said that all politics is local. Sorry, Tip, but any local government that bundled misfeasance, malfeasance and nonfeasance into such an ineffectual package would be driven from office this very evening.

Washington's logjam of problematical old business cannot be addressed by mere political promises. Most of these problems in fact are political promises run amok—the $16-trillion-and-growing national debt being the perfect example. The 537 men and women we elect to national office fiddled while these problems reached critical mass. Now these politicians have the power to let 320 million Americans enter the new epoch and compete…or the power to be 537 dinosaurs dragging us into history's tar pit.

I want to be an optimist about which choice our elected officials will make, but my experience watching politicians at work—most especially *groups* of politicians at work—suggests all bets should be hedged. The first company I founded was operating successfully in five countries when I divested my interest. Earlier, as an executive for another company, I conducted corporate business in several nations—often establishing that company's footprint in a new global outpost. I have been a guest lecturer at major universities in Scotland, the Netherlands, and Germany. I have enjoyed decades of world travel and observation, and how can one observe a place without observing its politics? In one of the most beautiful regions on earth, my native land, I have stayed in touch with friends and associates struggling endlessly in an effort to forge a competitive society and economy while their political institutions push in the opposite direction. In case you haven't guessed, Psarouthakis is a Greek name.

My observation has been that politicians, be they Greeks or Germans or Michiganders, share a pre-eminent trait. No matter what happens around them they will act to pursue their political interest, which primarily is to get elected. And re-elected. And re-elected again. If making a crucial decision would mean constituents must feel some pain (real or imagined), then that decision gets pushed aside. If an officeholder's constituents are split down the middle on a crucial issue, then that issue gets pushed aside. If it seems a crucial issue can be kicked down the road for years until the politician retires and someone else must deliver unwanted news to voters, then that issue gets ignored time and time again. If a crucial issue is one on which party leaders (and their re-election machine) demand a lockstep vote, then that issue gets a lockstep vote.

Traditionally, the "pressing" part of "this is a pressing issue" managed to get things accomplished in Washington. The fringes on left or right made their points, sometimes even serving as the cutting edge of progress. But the center would hold, common ground would be found, and the nation was governed. In recent years the political center has been overcome by a flood of ideological purity from either side, the eternal quest for re-election has become more time-consuming, and new media have put our politicians onstage every moment of the day. The result? Our government has become so dysfunctional one would think Washington is not the capital of the world's last superpower, but a Peter Sellers comedy set in one tiny duchy or another—except that, unlike a Peter Sellers movie, these people are not amusing. Each election day one hopes the lunacy has gone away and some business will get done. Instead, the new election cycle begins the day after the previous election cycle.

This manuscript was written in the first half of 2012, an

election year, a noisy time that only amplifies the irrational-
ity, the refusal to take serious business seriously, to a deafen-
ing level. One day, while thinking about how best to discuss
profound challenges raised by the new technological age and
the global economy, I took a break and turned on television
news. I found one political party's presidential contenders
bickering about birth control and the sitting president of the
United States squandering a ripe opportunity to move the nation toward energy self-sufficiency (mocking his supposedly
anti-green political foes while at the same time telling Brazil
to drill, baby, drill). No wonder the pundits often try to make
sense of this circus by asking who is the smart person in the
room–or, even more telling, who is the adult in the room?

Turning on TV news most anytime will also, within a minute or two, produce a politician chanting "Jobs! Jobs! Jobs!"
In today's climate that chant somehow passes for intelligent
discourse. It is not. It's political pandering, albeit effective
pandering, which is why both parties loudly indulge the same
chant. Of *course* we *all* want every American to have a livelihood and the best possible job. The real test of that chant has
nothing to do with political push-me, pull-you rhetoric about
whether the economy can best be grown by raising taxes or
by lowering taxes. The real test lies in the 21st Century vectors cited in this chapter's first paragraph—none of which can
be addressed until Congress and the White House clean up
their unfinished business. Keep in mind that image of a town
council playing and replaying "Groundhog Day." If any smart
adults are in that room they are in a minority, and clearly none
has the capacity to lead the kids in the room toward rational
action.

The future of American jobs, and fundamental change in
the workforce, is the ultimate subject of this book. In the end

you'll see that, in my view, the very words "jobs" and "job-lessness" will one day become archaic. Evolution can levy all the impact of revolution, and more. The great technological forces redesigning the workplace of our children and grand-children will trump every political slogan and chant, but we can adapt and prosper—unless Washington manages to choke our free market economy before it can evolve along with the new era. Sad to say, Washington is headed in that direction, in my opinion; and that too will be fodder for discussion later in these pages. But do hear this, which is not a matter of opinion: Our government's unfinished 20th Century business will, if left unfinished, drag the United States to the bottom of its poten-tial *no matter what political ideology holds sway in the future.*

"Political science" is a classic oxymoron. If science had produced this kind of wrong-headedness and dysfunction we would close all the nation's medical laboratories and hire witch doctors. If politicians are for the most part bright indi-viduals (and nearly all those whom I've met are bright people) ...and if they enter office with public service in mind (and I have no doubt that the overwhelming majority do exactly that) ...then how can they possibly be so distracted from compel-ling issues that will shape our future—theirs, yours, mine, and all Americans yet to be born?

How could Washington become so distracted from finish-ing trillions of dollars worth of relatively clear-cut old busi-ness so as to get on with an exciting and challenging and vital new era? It's as if our national legislators have never heard about these things, which is even crazier than the gridlock they embrace. The core 21st Century issues of which I speak are not exactly news. I do not claim to have discovered any of them. This is not the first book (or the 10th or the 20th) written by someone who has spent years thinking about these subjects. It is impossible to imagine more than a handful of Congress members making their way to our capital without at least having heard these issues discussed in serious tones by people they respect. So just what is the great distraction down in the District of Columbia anyway?

The allure of power is one obvious narcotic. Serious perks come with high office. There aren't enough hours in the day to talk to the glad-handers, lobbyists, ordinary citizens, and vote-counting colleagues seeking your ear. You are a big-time player back home, when you manage to get back there. And look—there you are on CNN! It's easy to envision such a picture. Power-tripping no doubt does play an important role in this morass. But such matters can't be quantified; and I have personally known politicians who remained civil, grounded, and respectful despite all this adulation, be it well-meant or mere fawning. Surely all but the weakest handful of politicians will emerge from any power trance long enough to hear intelligent warnings about serious work to be done.

A more important distraction, I think, is money. Not bribes, but dollars to lubricate the path toward that pre-eminent political goal, re-election. The contemporary officeholder spends more time raising campaign money than pursuing any other objective. Campaign treasuries must reach a very high number before a winning number of votes can be counted. If each politician's total revenue were tallied the way a service industry counts billable hours, it would be very easy to connect the dots. Speeches, lunches, photo ops, trips, long phone calls stroking big donors, strategy sessions with staff (the *political* staff)…these are the billable hours that produce the cash that pays for political Job One: re-election. It has become a colossal cost of doing business. Even the guy who wins the biggest job, the one that comes with a large white house and a briefcase that could destroy most of the world's population, incurs this cost of business. Sometimes even a president's own partisans are forced to throw their hands in the air and ask: "Is this the world's most powerful nation, or a small-town booster club raising money for ice hockey uniforms?" Considering what's at stake, it's not the money that's scary; it's the time spent raising it.

Counting campaign dollars is simple arithmetic. Public opinion polling, which is surpassed only by cold cash as the lifeblood of modern politics, involves more sophisticated math. To be fair, the office-holder does not spend time on a street corner asking the questions himself, perhaps only because poll respondents don't write checks. Hired pollsters do the dirty work, discovering what percentage of an office-holder's constituency own a hybrid car, believe the economy is more important than "the right to choose," have an unemployed family member, live in the suburbs, own a gun, think "the country is on the right (or wrong) track," and vow they will vote in the upcoming primary election. Asking such questions scientifically seems to account for all the science in political science. None of the questions has much to do with running the country effectively, but a lot to do with making the candidate's fund-raising dollars add up and keep flowing.

Endless polls spice a simmering stew stirred aimlessly by the politicians and 24/7 media, which ladle it out to a public that embraces "news as entertainment." News stories on any topic—natural disasters, school bus crashes, celebrity divorces, drug busts—produce sound bites for a day or two, then disappear. Politics gives the news-as-entertainment machine an added bonus in that, like sports, politics has winners and losers. Elections are held only every two years (and the heavyweight title fight every four years), but pollsters and politicians hell-bent for re-election make it possible to turn on the cameras and put the combatants in the ring *every single day!* In a two-party representative democracy this template becomes a sad spectacle. Here comes the political gladiator, wearing his or her party's talking points like boxing gloves. The other guy will be along in a minute. Punch. Punch. Punch. The idea of taking off the gloves and getting something accomplished before the next election has become a nostalgia piece.

Half a century ago Newton Minnow, John F. Kennedy's FCC chairman, declared network television programming to be a "vast wasteland." That was at a time when commercial television included live drama, Walter Cronkite was hosting programs like "Eyewitness to History," and Edward R. Murrow was completing his storied career with CBS. One is tempted to suggest that despite the addition of several hundred channels, the biggest TV wasteland of all can be found in today's concurrent obsession with, and diminution of, American politics.

Back in the dull days when most people had their news delivered in ink rather than pixels, it would have been laughable to float the idea of news becoming a broadcast entertainment commodity. The idea that Washington political news would draw the biggest crowds in the news-as-entertainment business would have been incomprehensible. The idea of a particularly entertaining or repugnant meaningless quote instantaneously going viral on the internet would have been, of course, science fiction. The idea of filling the seats at a political rally by tweeting an audience into existence would be laughable, incomprehensible *and* science fiction. But here we are.

Twitter traffic at this writing surpasses the equivalent of one 140-character message per day for every American—each message limited to the length of this sentence. People stroll through historic settings or alongside busy boulevards while looking at nothing but the screens of their portable electronic devices. Television news anchors, even as they talk to us in real time, urge us to *follow their tweets*. Our political institutions are not immune, becoming ever more glued to the moment and ever more distracted from smart, adult decisions that have long-term consequences. Living in the moment *might* provide a useful attitude adjustment for a given individual. For government, however, it is pure pathology. We need to know our history, and we need to take care of today's "In" basket. But good governance is about melding past and present experience into good stewardship of the future. As an excellent illustration, let's take a look at the nation's debt, a prime reason the United States can't get on with its future.

First, let me be clear that I am not some kind of zero-tolerance ideologue when it comes to debt, be it individual debt or corporate debt or sovereign debt. In the private sector I created two corporations by identifying and acquiring synergistic companies whose expertise and strengths fit my own business plans for growth. I came to know banks and bankers very well during this period, because borrowing money is a vital part of that endeavor. The money I borrowed from banks was one form of capital. It provided a means to grow an operation, create new wealth, save some jobs and create others, ultimately generating new capital to create still more new wealth. In that sense, corporate debt functions at the core of America's socioeconomic model, which is not a zero-sum system. We are all about growth, and growth is all about reasonable risks being taken—by lenders, by shareholders, and by the companies in which they invest capital.

With my own company's acquisitions, I defined "reasonable risk" as a maximum ratio of three times debt to equity. Soon after I began this company-building period of my career

in the 1980s, the go-go financial culture began offering higher, then *far* higher, debt ratios for the mere asking. Friends,
employees, and lenders themselves would say, "Hey, you can
borrow a lot more—why don't you?" My response was always a version, specific to each situation, of: "How are we
going to pay it back? Why go in debt so far that one bad-case
scenario would spell serious trouble? I am borrowing enough
to make the acquisition, set a course for growth, and pay back
the loan—or refinance the loan for still further growth. Why in
the world should I borrow more?" I sustained that philosophy
even as money became available at debt-to-equity ratios of
20/1, 30/1—and then soared even higher. Many companies,
needless to say, took the money. Many became supremely
sorry for doing so. Some did make a lot of money for themselves playing that game. No one ever denied you *might* make
a lot of money taking *un*reasonable risks.

Without trying to trace a timeline or draw detailed parameters, it is nonetheless clear that the financial meltdown of 2008
grew out of this culture. A culture of reasonable risk morphed
into a culture of unreasonable risk and, with new Wall Street
products and practices, flat-out gambling. It's not necessary
to attempt explaining the unexplainable market derivatives
and schemes that had nothing to do with generating new capital. Suffice it to say that the most basic American investment, the individual family home, routinely became a vehicle
of immense risk-taking. People who should not have been
given home mortgages, or at least not the mortgages they were
given, got them—just as foolhardy entrepreneurs could easily
enter grossly overleveraged business deals. These hopelessly
inflated and under-secured home mortgages were tied into
bundles of toxic paper disguised as equity products. These
bundles were then further inflated, and sold into the global

markets until they clogged financial seas like the swamps of plastic rubbish scientists lately have discovered in mid-ocean.

This toxic mortgage epidemic, at its initial point of infection, had a cheerleader: federal government policy regarding expanded home ownership, and the freewheeling translation of that policy by the neither-here-nor-there entities known as Fannie Mae and Freddie Mac. It is important to remember this when discussing federal regulation of the private-sector economy. Trust me when I tell you that unreasonable over-regulation is an anchor around the neck of business activity. Trust me when I tell you that the places where "just enough regulation" is needed tend to be rather apparent. And remember that their quasi-governmental charters make Fannie and Freddie perfect examples of why Washington should never be a *player* in free markets.

So, speaking as a former private-equity capitalist, let me assure you that finding some debt on our government's balance sheet does *not* bother me. The appearance of red ink is not in itself the reason our nation is financially crippled, vulnerable to deep and sudden crisis, and becoming more so every day. Precisely speaking, it is not even the raw amount of our sovereign debt that endangers all of us and, by rational expectation, should shame our elected officials into action. I say this although $16 trillion of red ink is a fearsome raw amount of debt. As with any borrower, what matters is the realistic proportion of debt on the balance sheet. Our sovereign debt has surpassed our entire Gross Domestic Product. That eye-popping yardstick and worse—inevitable with a GDP that refuses to grow by three percent a year while our debt grows at 10 percent—puts us very much on track to become a second-tier nation. That is the kind of balance sheet that should bother anyone. Even our yawning elected officials.

As an optimist I know how to look at the 2008 financial upheaval and note that the United States has not collapsed, most people still go to work each morning, baseball games will be played in summer and football in the fall, and there is no rioting in the streets. I do tend to look at the long term. I tend to favor the center of politics and opinion. I analyze trends and propositions on balance. But as a young engineer designing construction projects, I learned something about planning for tornadoes and floods and earthquakes. One does not say, "Two tons of steel and three tons of concrete will keep this structure standing against the highest winds and deepest floods anyone has seen around here in a long time." One designs structures to withstand something far worse, as well as the ravages of time, to say nothing of possible minor errors in one's own projections.

Our sovereign debt has been allowed to reach such a dangerous level that a *foreseeable* wind could take our economy down. Furthermore, the debt level is growing, despite political promises to repair damage inflicted by previous political promises. Our foreseeable catastrophic situation comes closer to our actual situation every day. Any engineer who designed our national balance sheet would be decertified, and then prosecuted for public endangerment. Yet, in the news-as-entertainment culture, a congressman texting lurid photos of himself will consume the news cycle's entire oxygen supply for days on end, until new infotainment can be found. Our nation's fiscal integrity ranks at the top of Washington's "old business," but at this writing has not generated any real buzz. Maybe that's because fiscal integrity is neither telegenic nor titillating. Maybe it's because the idea of entitlement reform seems to bring out the coward, or at least the master procrastinator, in every politician. What adjective best combines "sad," "amazing" and "frightening"?

Who knows in precisely what circumstances and at what debt-to-GDP ratio a crisis would be triggered in the cost of money, or at what point the government would begin printing more and more dollars for no reason except to create inflation and "monetize the debt"—an outcome that would let the government off the hook while paralyzing almost everyone else? The answer is, "No one knows." Not precisely. Some experts, from both left and right, foresee a near-term catastrophe. Others see a little more gas left in the tank. Almost all see the red fuel light flashing a bright warning. The politicians either ignore it, or respond with ideological sound bites. Paying for the things one buys while buried in debt is always a good way to attack a debt crisis. But politicians deep into one ideology refuse to impose tax increases of any kind upon anyone. Politicians deep into the other ideology pretend a soak-the-rich tax policy will balance the books (it won't; not even close) and is somehow "fair" (fair or not it certainly is a way of lining up enough votes to approach political job #1—staying in office).

President Obama created a bipartisan commission tasked with finding a debt solution. One could say the president farmed out the dirty work to someone else, rather than taking a clear leadership role. Or one could say he set up a mechanism for trying to get a solution to this crisis recast as a bipartisan effort. In any case, the commission came back with recommendations that would only have provided breathing space before judgment day. Nonetheless Congress members and senators representing both ideologies rejected the recommendations as too drastic. The president then thanked the commissioners for their work and sent them home. Nothing got passed but time.

My point is *not* to suggest specific steps toward solving

our "debt problem." It is to ask, "How did we get here, and why can't we get past this bad place?" I would begin answering my own question by complaining once again that no adults seem to be in the room. Our nation must cut back its appetites in most areas of the federal budget, some more than others. Such prioritizing must be more extensive than you might think because, despite record spending and debt, some vital needs are being ignored. We need to allocate money for those needs, and spend it, even as we prioritize and chop at waste. On the other side of the ledger we need to increase revenues. In the long term, economic growth will do that trick. In the short run we must be careful not to cripple the economy. In the government sector, that means we cannot impose a balanced budget next week and it means we cannot seek to cut every tax on the books. We need to get serious about reinventing the U.S. Tax Code, an obvious big step toward a solution that will not step on any honest ideologue's toes. Such reform would reveal in an instant that "revenue enhancement" does not always mean a tax increase.

Standing awestruck at the sight of such a dysfunctional government, let me suggest that one must deploy—in a disciplined fashion—procedures favored, with no discipline at all, by both opposing ideologies. We must cut, a lot. We must spend, a lot. We must live within our means, but we must also track toward growth with a reasonable debt-to-equity ratio. Isn't that what smart adults do in the budgeting process? It's what good corporations do. It is what good government must do.

Amid all the ideological political posturing leading nowhere, when is the last time you heard a serious political plea for answering our national infrastructure needs? My fellow engineers are on record insisting we need *$2 trillion* worth of repairs and upgrades in the next five years—a tab that will become still more expensive if delayed. We spend only half as much of our GDP on infrastructure as does Europe, and less than a third of what China is now spending. Yet our lawmakers can maneuver their way through a stump speech or a town meeting without once mentioning the word "infrastructure." How could this be? Could it be that every single American would benefit from a wide-ranging repair and upgrade of our highways and airports and water supply and sewage systems and other key engineered pieces of our shared civilization, and therefore getting that job done would not produce an edge at the ballot box? That's so cynical I don't offer it for serious speculation. The thought does reflect my amazement that the greatest nation on earth has allowed its public works projects, as infrastructure used to be called, to fall into second-tier quality.

The unaddressed infrastructure problem illustrates that, yes, there is not merely a place but a need for federal "investing in our future." That is a very politically charged phrase. Many politicians advocate government "investment" in ways with which I would quarrel strongly. To cite one example, it is dumbfounding that the federal government would reach so far afield from basic research (something it rightly and effectively can support) as to indulge in stock-picking—which essentially is what the Energy Department did when it gave Solyndra its infamous half-billion-dollar loan. The bureaucrats exercised such poor due diligence that taxpayers took a savage haircut. That's an example of government "investing" as a sin. Failing to put the Keystone Pipeline on a fast track from Canada was an equally dumbfounding sin in the opposite direction. Government could have made a significant and timely "investment in our future" just by getting out of the way. Failure to do so was an excellent illustration of regulation by politics instead of regulation along a reasonable channel that is vital to our American economy.

Our country is virtually insolvent (no other entity can borrow money all day and all night with near impunity and then, when that strategy goes badly, as it must, print devalued money to pay the bills). This sovereign debt situation *is* a crisis, and it *must* be solved if we are to achieve any of the things this book wishes to talk about. So why only one chapter focusing on our crippling debt and our crippled government? Two reasons.

First, the debt is best addressed more deeply and specifically by commentators with other areas of interest and expertise. Second, the debt is an easier problem to solve than the menu of 21st Century issues that comprise THE TECHNOLOGY IMPERATIVE. Let me explain.

Almost everyone knows we cannot allow the national debt to continue spiraling into the stratosphere. The phrase "unsustainable debt" has become a cliché in political discourse. It is not a secret. The only thing needed solve the debt problem is a collective will to pass laws and make the problem go away. Easy for me to say. But that is the *entire* task: finding the will. Yes, the necessary legislation and policy changes will have painful political consequences, both in program cuts and tax increases. It's also true that the tiniest encampment in the most remote area of the Nevada desert would barely increase in size if we sent to that place every educated American who doesn't understand the need to make adjustments in both spending *and* revenues. Still, nothing happens.

The traditional way of making things happen amid gridlock is leadership, and leadership traditionally has been the province of the executive branch. That leg of our tripod government falls on the shoulders of just one man. It seems unfair; but leadership by committee has seldom made the history books.

One of my life's heroes was a haberdasher from a small Missouri town who found himself in the world's most important leadership position. Without pause he went straight to the work of leading. Harry Truman ordered atomic bombs dropped on Hiroshima and Nagasaki. Historians will, in the comfortable distance of retrospect, argue forever about the wisdom of that decision. Truman created the post-war Marshall Plan that saved Europe from peacetime destitution and anarchy. He promulgated the "Truman Doctrine," which saved Turkey and Greece from Soviet opportunism. He took the first steps toward integrating the U.S. armed services. His decisiveness generated intense criticism from various quarters at various times, to which he responded by saying those who can't stand the heat should get out of the kitchen. Harry Truman probably would have detested rock and roll, but a famous rock band nonetheless wrote a song entitled "Harry Truman," a tune dripping with nostalgia for his direct honesty. And mostly, I would say, his leadership.

At this writing, and possibly for four more years, our president is a man who came to office young, inexperienced, clearly very bright, and clearly lacking leadership qualities. A prime example in his first term would be health-care reform. Except for a few demagogues, Americans understand that our health-care system needs some kind of reform. It is too expensive, too many people fail to receive adequate care or preventive medicine or both, and its extraordinary cost inflation is a huge burden on our economy. America scores poorly on many important global health statistics such as low birth weight babies for many reasons, but not all of these failures fall strictly on the people and institutions who deliver care. The quality of our health-care research and education is unsurpassed, as is our best specialized care. It is a mixed report card.

Anyone who refused to admit, as Barack Obama took office, that our health-care system needed repair was either not paying attention or was wed to near-religious belief that "messing with our health care" is treasonous. Such a belief system is not to be taken lightly. Attempts at health-care reform have seldom gone well, except when the candy-store approach to government debt—as in the Bush II administration's bipartisan expansion of Medicare prescription benefits—gives politicians cover for a bank-busting program.

I single out health care for these few extra paragraphs because if ever there is a place where leadership is needed, it is in trying to pass major, complex legislation on a topic with deeply entrenched partisan opposition on either side of its many components. Elements of reform must be laid out separately and clearly, and their rationale must be cemented into sustainable support from most Americans. Bill Clinton turned the task over to his wife, who tried to get the job done via a committee whose membership shunned the health-care professions, did its work in secret, then wondered why its recommendations fell on the table with a resounding thud. When it came Barrack Obama's turn, instead of leading the task he turned it over to Nancy Pelosi, his House speaker, to proceed much as she and the House Democratic leadership saw fit. Two years later Obamacare was law—but as a result the House belonged to the other party, the Supreme Court was hearing arguments on Obamacare's constitutionality, and in any case so many Americans oppose the law that it will be a political football for the foreseeable future.

Whether President Obama gains a second term, or someone else has moved into the White House as you read these words, we all should hope or pray (or editorialize or deploy whatever exhortation mechanism we prefer) for much stronger leadership. Unfair as it may be to put such a heavy load on the person living on Pennsylvania Avenue, the leadership burden always has landed at that address, in the kitchen known as the Oval Office. I take the liberty of talking here about the political atmosphere of the 24/7 media age not because I see any handy way of changing it, but because it makes presidential leadership all the more important. More than ever, the president must be smart, must be adult, must be in the room, and must find a way to garner significant points of agreement from both sides of our widening political gulf. That is a tall order, and at times might seem impossible. But it is likely to be the only way forward.

Most of all, this chapter was written because Washington's old 20th Century business must be cleared from our agenda before we can meaningfully confront the new technological age and global economy. All best wishes to our elected officials as *they* write the end to this chapter, as only they can do. America's successful entry into the 21st Century depends on their performance. It is entirely possible that whoever writes the next *Brave New World* will note that 2013—for good or bad—was the year the United States determined its role in the tale.

CHAPTER TWO

Opportunity and irreversible truths

I came to the United States from Crete carrying almost no baggage except a surname most Americans find difficult to pronounce. It was 1951. I had $15 in my pocket, a few words of English, and a naïve determination to study at a great engineering school. My "Boston aunt" had recommended a particular school known worldwide by its initials, which I assumed would be pronounced as one word: "Mitt." I soon learned to say "Em Eye Tee." I did not anglicize "Psarouthakis." In time almost everyone—friends, colleagues, new acquaintances—began avoiding the surname problem by calling me "Dr. John." Very informal. Very democratic. Very American.

How could I possibly not love this country? I was an orphan raised by penniless aunts in a poor Mediterranean neighborhood. In America I received a world-class education, did research in an exotic niche of the U.S. space program, entered the private sector as a technology manager, moved to the business side, learned how to evaluate underachieving companies and how to acquire them. Riding the American Dream as far as possible, I founded my own manufacturing firm and grew it into a Fortune 500 company with units in Italy, Germany, Japan, and the UK as well as the United States. In busy semi-retirement I have written books, promoted cultural exchange programs, done some adjunct university teaching near my Michigan home, and am now commuting to Europe three times a year as a guest lecturer at one of the world's oldest and finest universities. It has been a long, wonderful journey from that adobe bungalow, without running water, where I grew up.

I tell you these things not to brag. My point aims in the opposite direction. I am one among *millions* of immigrants who stepped off the boat and flourished in a country unlike any other. No nation has presented such fertile opportunity for hyphenated citizens, Greek-Americans and German-Americans and Italian-Americans and Irish-Americans and Arab-Americans and Mexican-Americans and Chinese-Americans...the list spans the globe. In time, even hyphenated Americans brought here under the most heinous human condition, slavery, have seen opportunity extend to the #1 job in the land. America remains imperfect, as it always has been and always will be. But the United States also remains the last best hope for humanity, a true nation of immigrants, the world's destination of choice. If heaven is best defined as "the place people want to go," then America is the world's once and (I hope) future heaven on earth.

Right now, though, we and all the world's nations are converging upon an era that already has produced momentous, indelible change. Everyone realizes the earth has rapidly become a global village. I am not sure how many realize we have barely reached the outskirts of a technological age that will differ more radically from the 20th Century than Columbus's "New World" differed from 15th Century Spain. This should be a good time, an *exciting* time to be alive. This should be the near-perfect year for a Greek-American scientist, technologist, corporate manager, and entrepreneur to become an octogenarian and write about what he has seen thus far in life. It hasn't worked out that way. The free-market economy that made America a unique beacon of opportunity faces grave imminent danger. With the economy stagnant, the political vultures are circling. Class warfare is in the air. Our young people are finding no smooth path toward a livelihood, even as they are being asked to pay the entitlements tab imposed by a soaring retiree-to-employee ratio. One seldom sees or hears the phrase "the American Dream."

This is no way to confront the challenges of a radically new world. Bolstering America's essential character of economic freedom and entrepreneurial independence is our only hope of competing, flourishing, and leading. Too many politicians, however, entered the 21st Century making familiar promises propped up by old realities, all the while misusing the finite share of our economy that is available for governance. After leading us to the brink of bankruptcy, and doing nothing to repair the damage, their gridlock only *seems* to sustain the status quo. The truth is our government, like sourdough, keeps growing even when left unattended. I fear current trends will choke our great economic engine so badly that an anxious citizenry will chase phony solutions still further in the wrong direction. Because our free-market economy served us so well for so long, big-government salesmen will need a whale-sized red herring to close the deal—but they might have found one. If voters do not understand technology's role in workplace upheaval, then the new global economy will absolutely scare them to death. The GDP-sized question is this: Are American voters so scared they'll blindly vote to kill the goose that, when healthy, lays *everyone's* golden eggs?

If the U.S. slips ever deeper into a government dependency model, this country will no longer be exceptional—let alone unique. We will lose not just the energy and creativity that newcomers have brought to this shore for many generations. We will lose the reason they have always clamored to get here. We will become not a nation attracting immigrants, but a nation generating emigrants. Upending America's place in the world's imagination is a prospect that shocks and angers any "newcomer" who, like me, has been an American longer than the average American has been alive. I have no doubt that the phrase "land of opportunity" has been misused, over-used, and abused—but of all the descriptive titles bestowed on the United States, it is the best and most accurate. It says why so many millions of us came here, and it says opportunity is a precious commodity. It says those who aspired to come here, compared with those who acquired opportunity just by being born here, tend to understand opportunity better and value it higher. "The American spirit" is far more vague, and open to endless interpretations. Best perhaps to nail it down by saying: "The American spirit is something that arises in the world's foremost *land of opportunity*."

Have we become too "sophisticated" for that kind of talk? Is that why such phrases seem to have disappeared? Maybe. Sicily-born Frank Capra's movies wouldn't sell in today's movie theaters, but few meaningful or inspirational films do. Did Lee Iacocca's second-generation sense of America guide his terrific work in restoring Ellis Island? I have no doubt. Perhaps I am wrong in believing this key thread of the American persona has been slipping from sight, we are the worse for it, and this helps explain why no one seems able to rally and lead in a time demanding hard choices. Or perhaps I am correct.

In any case, here we sit, the world's great free-market economy, badly in need of some fine-tuning to meet the demands of a new tech-driven universe. But this economy must simultaneously cope with a government that swallows all the GDP it can grab, spends its revenue with stunning inefficiency, inhibits business growth with regulatory sins of both commission and omission, increasingly misjudges which things it can do very well and which things it can only do very badly, and—from many quarters, including the current White House—wants to blame most of our society's ills on the population segment that pays the bulk of federal income taxes.

If high blood pressure is the silent killer of the human body, and can be detected by a simple meter, then countless simple metrics have been warning us about the silent stalker of our prosperity. For example, federal transfer payments as a percentage of Americans' personal income have quietly *doubled* in just the last four decades, and continue to grow. In recent years, almost none of the increase in transfer-payment income has gone to the lowest-income Americans. These two facts, individually and in their stunning overlap, are worth a moment of silent reflection. Just how high can a house of cards be built? Who is going to pay for it? THE TECHNOLOGY IMPERATIVE will demand the very best and most competitive goods and services that societies, economies, and *individuals* around the world can offer. This is a time to be strengthening, not weakening, our free-market and limited-government dynamic. After all, we now hope to be entering a *world* of opportunity.

When the dust clears, the United States might yet remain the globe's leading economy. We might be in position to sustain the largest *per-capita* economy as far into the future as the eye can see. That will be up to the politicians, the pundits, and the policymakers. And, of course, the people. But great crises tend to be best resolved only in the presence of great leadership. Our crisis of debt and government-by-promissory-note will be solved only after the accumulated problem is fully revealed and comprehended by all, like lifting Oz's curtain... and credible solutions are laid out ...and a solid majority is inspired to follow or get out of the way while we dig out. More difficult missions on short deadlines—winning a world war, going to the moon—are stock in trade for this country when it has great leadership.

This time, after mobilizing enough public resolve to clear 20th Century old business off the table (or more realistically, after charting a clear, guaranteed, orderly transition to that end), our president and those elected and private-sector leaders who choose to join him will face an even larger challenge. We must play instant catch-up and put the United States on course to compete and prosper in a new world. Another decade of ideological politics and demagoguery would generate disaster, followed by chaos, followed by something worse. That's my non-partisan assessment. An ideologue leader from the left would tack toward governance in which *most* personal income is distributed via federal transfer payment, regulatory zeal stifles growth, and a zero-sum economic game can only be sustained by printing funny money. An ideologue leader from the right would tack toward governance that blindly atrophies its own muscle at every opportunity, cuts taxes without regard for any goal but an instantly balanced budget, and forgoes *good* government investments (think infrastructure and basic research). Choose your poison. Either would be fatal.

This is not a political book. The one tenet I hold as absolute has been portrayed lately as right-leaning political bedrock, which it is not. It is to me an obvious non-partisan truth, one embraced by John F. Kennedy *and* Ronald Reagan, the two most revered American political leaders, left and right, of my adult life. The tenet, which underlies every sentence in this book, is this: *I believe our free-market economy is the cornerstone of American prosperity—the engine that allows each of us the opportunity to thrive as we pursue happiness.*

I oppose any politics that asserts otherwise. And there you have the full extent of my political orthodoxy. I am otherwise very much a political centrist. Unless you are very young, by the way, you understand that "the center" is a movable place. Thankfully so. If, for example, the center were positioned today as it was 100 years ago, American women would not be allowed to vote.

It would be nice to see a little more—no, a lot more—centrism in American politics and American society. I think we all would settle right now for effective leadership. My only immutable, non-negotiable requirement for a leader is that he or she, Republican or Democrat, young or old, signs on to fully support and protect not just our great Constitution, but that italicized sentence above. That'll work.

The federal government's incompetent stewardship of our financial future as the 21st Century rushed toward us and then as the calendar turned has brought the United States very near, in my opinion, a point of no return. Our new challenges form a mosaic of great complexity, from the largest multinational enterprise to details as tiny as a three-person business or 10-student community-college classroom somewhere in the Heartland (as we here in Michigan prefer to call Flyover Country). Nonetheless, every particle of this living mosaic derives from those four benchmark vectors cited in the first paragraph of Chapter One: technological innovation, global economic competition, education reform, and a new paradigm for the manufacturing sector. Is there anyone who does not realize that whether the United States soars to new heights or sinks into mediocrity will be defined by how we perform in those four areas? An infinite number of problems and possibilities will require smart decisions and agile execution. Some will present legitimate fodder for debate.

A sketch of these conjoined benchmarks has been apparent for a very long time. The first IBM personal computer had not yet been delivered when wise old shop-floor workers could be heard lamenting: "We'll never survive if this country quits making things! Nobody will have a job!" They were on the right track, throughout the years of an alleged "service economy" and on into "the IT economy." The smokestacks quit belching in their mid-20th Century profusion long ago, but a vibrant American economy without a vibrant manufacturing sector is simply impossible. It will come down to how smart we are in choosing what we manufacture, how we manufacture those things, and what those 21st Century factories can generate for our economy and our society besides the products themselves.

The floor becomes littered with obvious questions. The most compelling inquiry might go something like: If this challenge is bigger than the 1960s space program, and if it is vital to our survival, why hasn't it fully engaged the public imagination? Talking heads and "news" programming fill the air around the clock, so why aren't these issues approached in depth rather than the mere politics of it? Why are even the politics so shallowly covered and simplistically understood? ("Jobs! Jobs! Jobs!" does not qualify as insight.) Why hasn't the full dynamic of our simultaneously exciting and frightening *tomorrow* attracted a more visible and meaningful public dialogue *today*? Are science and technology and economics and, yes, the business community just too unsexy to compete with show biz, sports, video game apps, and the aforementioned congressman getting stupid with his "smart" phone? We are after all talking about the quality of American life (including the ability to buy movies tickets, big TV screens, and smart phones).

Those are excellent questions. When infotainment drowns out high-priority matters of substance, people need to shout the right stuff straight into the dialogue. Political leaders and would-be leaders and policy wonks and talking heads and educators at every level long ago should have begun standing up to say, forcefully:

"We must position ourselves to excel in these four 21st Century arenas right now. We need to address these issues with sweeping, fundamental change or we will be toast. These are not our only challenges. Sad to say, we also have to deal with enormous chronic and worsening problems caused by bad choices made right here in Washington. A runaway debt reaching to the moon and back. A growing reliance on government, to the point that *our government itself is a prisoner of government's reliance on government.* Our infrastructure is crumbling, having been neglected for decades while entitlement spending soared. Our government collects dollars by the scores of billions, but all the cash goes straight back out the door without covering our expenditures. We need to borrow nearly half of every dollar we spend. These criticisms are not politics-speak. They are *survival*-speak.

"Even as we take care of these past mistakes we must stay ahead of the world in technology, because *innovation* is our most valuable export…we must retain a competitive manufacturing capacity in value-added products…we must create an educational mind-set that prepares our advanced college graduates to do the R&D and our junior-college graduates to produce those value-added products…and unless we do all of this with *global* reach and competitiveness every step of the way…then you can forget about the United States as a world leader. You can forget about growing our economy. You can forget about a prospering citizenry. It won't be so bad that you will want to move to Bangladesh. But many other countries will start looking real good to those of you who are able to get there, and who are lucky enough to be allowed in if you try."

Those two paragraphs are approximately the length of Lincoln's Gettysburg Address. If merely most of what they say is true (and I believe every word is true—with the first sentence being as reliable as Newton's law), then a good speechwriter has the raw material for the political speech our nation needs so desperately to hear through all the din.

It's prudent to be skeptical whenever you hear someone shout "fire!" on the pages of a book. Each day's passing scene and entire chunks of history are filled with gloom-and-doom predictions that go bust, and with "storms of the century" that could have been waited out. But here's a hard truth I encountered in a physics course as a very young MIT undergraduate. I learned a weighty English word, and was confronted with a weighty law of physics—and of life. The word is "irreversible." It's not a difficult word. Its meaning is clear. The physical law, however, reaches beyond profound. I stopped in my tracks to ponder it. Some things are reversible. Some things cannot be reversed. Not just as a philosophical concept, but irreversible in the molecules of the real world in which we live, enjoy liberty and pursue happiness.

Sorting "reversible" from "irreversible" thus becomes crucial to the policymaking process. It is the first important thing to understand about this global, technology-driven economy that has begun visiting *irreversible* change upon us. We cannot wait out this storm. It won't go away. No pendulum swing of a business cycle or political majority, or simple passage of time, will see us through. No genie can be put back in the bottle. We need to acknowledge the irreversible quality of this new age, accept its negative impact on our obsolete strengths, embrace its positive areas of potential, shift our focus to our positive strengths, and find ways to prevail in global competition.

I imagine that by now *everyone* believes, privately at least, that the United States as we know it cannot endure and prosper unless it embraces the global economy and learns how to compete in that arena. Some of us, however, have serious disagreements about how to do so. My own view says it is ludicrous, and ultimately catastrophic, to think we can grow the economy by growing the government. For those who believe otherwise, let me suggest that it is one thing to distribute wealth and consume wealth; it is something altogether different to *create* wealth.

No two developed nations have followed the same path toward capitalism or toward free markets. No country's economic system is "pure." One should note, in fact, that the two great bastions of Cold War communism, the former Soviet Union and China, have now arrived at different points along their experimental path with markets that are somewhat free. This welcome process has finally gotten at least a foothold (and in China's case a very large foothold) because descendants of Leninists and Maoists are learning that—hello!—distributing wealth without creating wealth is the path to bread lines. Capitalism, meanwhile, is one thing in Germany and another thing in the UK and another thing in Singapore. Numerous nations are successful capitalist nations. None, however, practiced a version of capitalism that excelled like the

American version, not with a scope so large as to draw a template for the world and to evolve the world's currency.

Now, it has become painfully evident that America's capitalist paradigm needs retooling. It has become less efficient at providing a livelihood for the citizenry. We have a serious unemployment problem and an even more serious underemployment problem. Our middle class has been hammered and has, in fact, been the focus of most new reliance on government entitlements. Income for a majority of Americans has stagnated. The private sector is not "the cause" of all that, but the American brand of capitalism clearly has not performed in the manner to which we have become accustomed. We must fix that. We must do so before populist politics and an entitlement mentality fly past that point of no return. We need to be smart, and we need to be quick about it.

We need to get serious about entering a global, technology-driven, free-market competitive world with a government that does not believe it should decide which green energy companies deserve capitalization, and thinks it better to let Canadian oil flow to China than to the United States. Some nations have always had a larger government finger in the pie, and we have always beaten them in economic competition We will continue to beat them, including the major new players, if we make necessary efforts in all four benchmark vectors. If most everyone understands that fact, then why—aside from that nagging need to clean up 20th Century problems, and a failure in communicating the story—aren't we moving forward?

We all know where the continental divide lies, ideologically speaking. One ideology is dominated by those who believe soaking the rich and pretending debt has no consequences will, as they endlessly proclaim, "Get the country back on track again." The other ideology is dominated by those who believe cutting taxes and slashing federal spending will auto-matically fire up the economic engine and, as they also end-lessly proclaim, "get the country back on track again." We need somehow to eliminate such ideological Puritans from the political circus. Otherwise, whichever ideology most suc-cessfully panders to the largest number of voters will always prevail. That is why demagogues on the left have moved so near to pushing the United States still further away from a (relatively) free-market economy, and away from a (rela-tively) limited-government model. Not much farther down that path our gooses will be cooked, golden egg and all. Your goose, my goose, my political enemy's goose, my political friend's goose.

The electorate has never voted for inconvenience, or the mere mention of pain—let alone pain itself. In 2008 at a Michigan campaign stop, John McCain made an offhand statement of obvious fact, referring to high-wage industrial jobs that had disappeared in and around the automobile in-dustry. "Some of these jobs aren't coming back," McCain said. Imagine that—painful truth cluttering a political stump speech! Within a few days McCain removed his campaign staff from Michigan, conceded the presidential primary elec-tion, and his White House aspirations were doomed. Flash forward to February 2011 and a private banquet in Silicon Valley. President Obama asked Steve Jobs what it would take to make iPhones in America instead of China. Steve Jobs replied, according to a dinner guest interviewed by the New York Times: "Those jobs aren't coming back." If gold stars were awarded for irony dripping from nearly identical quotes, few would shine so brightly.

Yes, as we hemorrhage jobs, it would be nice if Apple's iconic electronic device *du jour* were made by American workers. But we can't waste money or time fighting losing battles against irreversible tides. We must identify winnable battles, and go win them. The United States can only compete in a global economy by reclaiming and enhancing a clear lead as the world's innovator. This can only be done if we continue to develop leading-edge technology and sustain crucial value-added manufacturing operations. In the new technological age this will require a sort of "just-in-time" educational establishment providing workers with necessary skills. And there we are, as will happen in almost any discussion about important elements of America's future, right back at those vital, synergistic benchmark vectors.

Instead of killing our free-market golden goose, even if it currently is laying somewhat tarnished eggs and not enough of them, let's give it room to breathe and let's nurse it back to health. Let's teach it how to grow and prevail again. *That* is the only way to get this train and its 320 million passengers back on track. It's the only way we can be, and the only way we ever were, the land of opportunity.

CHAPTER THREE

It's the technology, stupid

Technology is neither good nor evil. It is neither progressive nor regressive. It is whatever we—individuals, communities, nations, the global economy—make of it, positive or negative or both. The internet, for example, has done more than any religion or any language or any empire in world history to put humans in touch with each other. That's a breathtaking superlative no one can deny. A citizen of a backward dictatorship in some forlorn corner of the world can—given a handheld device and internet access—communicate in real time with, say, expatriate groups in San Francisco or London. Simultaneously. Hooray for the internet. On the other hand, the internet can disseminate more pornography in one day than all the world's printing presses have disseminated since Gutenberg bought his first barrel of ink.

The parallel trade-offs are endless. Our most advanced airplanes can carry people, or can carry weapons of mass destruction. A new medication can ease human misery, or can be diverted to the narcotics trade. Almost any new technology can be deployed in positive or negative ways. The choices are ours. But rest assured that the internet, modern aviation, and pharmaceutical research cannot and will not go away. Nor should they.

Decades ago I made the transition from government scientist to research-and-development director for a major private-sector manufacturer. From that day forward I began acquiring a deeper and deeper understanding of how competition drives prosperity and progress, and how new technology far more often than not lies at the center of the action. Let's pretend you own a company that produces machines used by other companies to make other products. Let's also pretend your flagship machine works well, and you have no competition. Your customers do not clamor for you to develop more efficient products, so you begin to believe your company is a perpetual motion machine disguised as a cash register. It doesn't work that way. Free markets will ferret out any void (in this case, your failure to innovate), and competition will fill that void. New technology is found and harnessed. Your market sector becomes continually more efficient, with you or without you. Competition drives this syndrome. New technology makes it possible. Absent a Soviet-style authoritarian state, movement along this channel of progress can be impeded but it cannot be stopped. Even an authoritarian state will, sooner or later, find itself penetrated by competition from outside, as surely as rainfall finds the sea.

But what about the connection between new, technology-driven efficiencies and our current employment problems—which are far more profound than any statistical "jobless rate" will ever reveal? Millions of smokestack jobs no longer exist. Millions of other American jobs, from nearly every sector, have been exported. Tens of millions of Americans are sustained only by the safety net, or by working multiple part-time jobs at low wages with no benefits. More than one-quarter of working Americans lack sufficient resources to sustain themselves three months if laid off, a number one imagines has worsened since it was last compiled. This is a very, very bad time to be an unskilled worker, an underskilled worker, or what one might call a "formerly skilled" worker. The link between this picture and technology is absolutely as direct as the fact that you haven't seen any elevator operators lately. This is the crux of our discussion here, really; because when *progress* takes away someone's livelihood, then progress has created low-hanging fruit for demagogues peddling big-government solutions. That is the non-competitive, no-growth, dead-end way of filling a void.

As dismal as the employment landscape might look, and as formidably challenging as the future might be, our new technological age is not unprecedented in terms of American workplace upheaval. I am not speaking of a financial crash, as in the Great Depression of the 1930s. I mean a time when new technology-driven efficiencies caused irreversible change, radically altering forever the face of daily life in the United States. If you have no job or no good job, you probably view such historical parallels as a distinction without a difference. But to put this newest new world in context while sizing up the task before us, it might be good to think about what happened to the American farm.

In the late 19th Century, more than half of American workers were employed on farms. Countless others earned their livelihoods selling goods to farmers or transporting and processing farm products. Today fewer than *two percent* of Americans work on farms. Meanwhile, our farms' productivity per acre, thanks to technology and mechanization, has soared. In 1940—not 1840, but *1940*—one American farmer's output fed 19 people for a year. By 1960, one farmer fed 61 people. Today's American farmer is estimated to feed, on average, more than 150 people. This startling transition was set in motion generations ago, meaning these statistics have lost the first-hand, breath-taking impact they had on your grandfather or great-grandfather as they lived through it.

Today's typical American is distinctly urban, not agricultural. He probably thinks of farmers (to the extent he thinks at all about a minuscule number of fellow citizens, whom he never sees) as being the *least* affected by technology. To the contrary, it takes a word larger than "enormous" to describe technology's impact on agricultural employment numbers and on skills required of those who still farm. Agriculture's statistical ships passing in the night—farm employment plunging, farm skill requirements soaring—eerily foreshadowed the transition we now see in manufacturing. And manufacturing, of course and ironically, is where the bulk of agricultural workers migrated across the first half of the 20th Century. Fortunately for all of us, it was a migration to the private sector, free markets, and therefore a path to economic growth.

Think about the scope of change that occurred in little more than 100 years, all of it driven by new technology. Our greatest 19th Century public engineering project spanned a vast continent with railroad tracks, allowing homesteaders to ship farm produce and livestock to our cities. Americans rode a horse, or used a horse to pull a carriage. Before the advent of mechanized harvesting equipment, Americans once fielded an eye-popping 22 million working animals. You know what happened in the next wave of technology. We now produce far, far more food per farmer, and per acre, than we did when most Americans were dedicated to producing and processing food. That is undeniable technology-driven progress, but it was accompanied by upheaval and fear and, for many, pain.

Our task early in the 21st Century is to make our latest technological upheaval turn out as well as when farmhands became factory workers. Back then the great American economic engine created a vast middle class, and "the American

Century" was born. That will not be an easy trick to replicate. In fact, in any exactly parallel sense it will be impossible. An unskilled farmhand will never again be able to walk onto an assembly line and sign on for a lifetime job at a wage that would provoke genuine jealousy among the middle class of any other nation, oil sheikdoms excepted. The 21st Century worker making an equivalent transition will need to work with his mind, and technical savvy, to an extent never before approached by a vast workforce.

In 1995, a dozen years before General Motors filed the largest manufacturing bankruptcy in U.S. history, I gave a speech to the Grand Rapids Economic Club. Michigan's second largest city, on the west side of the state, hubs an area with an economy somewhat distanced from the traditional boom-and-bust cycle of the car industry. In 1995, in fact, Grand Rapids and the university town Ann Arbor were the only Michigan cities that had recorded recent growth in real per capita income. Nonetheless, Michigan unemployment was the lowest it had been in decades—below the national average, believe it or not. By traditional measures the economy, in the state and nationally, was doing OK. In Grand Rapids, things were looking splendid. So when I described an urgent need to bolster our manufacturing sector by encouraging diversification, and by steering capital toward smaller companies—which usually are technology-based—a clear response of "if it ain't broke, why fix it?" filled the air. In fact, as I delivered my remarks about larger companies becoming centers of unemployment rather than centers of employment, I could see some polite eyeball-rolling among Michigan's Republican governor, John Engler (now president of the Business Roundtable), and his companions down front.

Here is part of what I said that day (italics added):

"I describe the economy in terms of two vectors. The first vector represents the very large corporations. They dominate their industries. In many cases such industries have a defined and developed market. If we use the American auto industry as an example, the market in this country, given a static population, is saturated. The only elasticity in demand is relative to consumers' decision to accelerate or postpone purchas...The drive for increased productivity through downsizing and increased automation are characteristic of companies in this vector. *These are companies that may generate wealth but are unlikely to generate new employment.*

"The second vector involves those companies, usually smaller, which are entrepreneurial-based, and which grow out of new and emerging technologies. These are companies which are creating new markets, new industries or sub-industries...(This vector) is much more employment growth-oriented. Companies in this vector, if they are successful, may see an explosion in their growth curve. Their growth is more likely to be exponential or geometric. *Companies in the first vector are looking for ways to reduce employment and enhance productivity. Companies in the second vector, as a function of their growth and their nature, are likely to add employees.* They need the human resources to build product or provide services to satisfy a newly created demand."

Not surprisingly, I didn't utter a single sentence about how technology revolutionized agriculture. It certainly would have been appropriate, though, to include a footnote on the biggest workplace upheaval in U.S. history to date. *Irrevers-ible* technological change always has a place while discussing the future. Audiences as recently as that day in 1995, however, were uncomfortable just to hear a successful auto-parts CEO talk about the need to regard the automotive Big Three as important *current* major employers, while urging more attention be paid to capital needs of emerging *future* employers.

This evolutionary vision of the workplace had been a ker-nel part of my thinking for a long time. It represented the overall tenor of my advice as chairman of the Michigan Strategic Fund, a board formed by Governor Jim Blanchard, John Engler's Democratic predecessor, to encourage technology-driven startup companies and diversify the state's economy. Blanchard appointed me to the Strategic Fund chairmanship in 1989. It was a perfect fit for my experience and my interests, and I gave it serious attention until Governor Engler took office and sent me a letter advising that my services were no longer needed. I was surprised, even though sweeping out a previous administration's appointees is standard political practice. I regard my own occasional public service as strictly apolitical. Over the years I have donated small amounts of cash to candidates and officeholders of both parties. I vote for whomever I regard as most qualified, then wish success to the winner. I had thought of Jim Blanchard as our governor, not as a Democrat.

My Grand Rapids speech centered on the need to nurture new centers of employment while old employment megaliths inevitably mature, stagnate as job creators, and then shrink their workforces. That, in other words, is why I urged "fixing something that ain't broke." The auto industry's jobs—any industry's jobs—were, and are, nothing to scoff at. But new technologies, new efficiencies, new consumer demands, and new products will *irreversibly* change any industry. So my counsel that day—and before, and since—said in essence: We need to ensure that capital flows to job-creating segments of the economy.

In some quarters "capital" has been reduced to a whisper word, at best. We are thankfully still a capitalist country, however, and capital is not merely a word for inspiring ideological food fights and sound bites. (Though I must say that "Capital! Capital! Capital!" comes nearer the mark than "Jobs! Jobs! Jobs!") Capital remains the tangible fuel that keeps our economic engine running, and the marketplace remains the only way to create new wealth, which is where all those new "jobs, jobs, jobs" must come from—even that lesser percentage of jobs that must be attached to a government paycheck. That's why the core of my dusty old Grand Rapids speech remains central to confronting our new technological age—unless, of course, one believes our prosperity can best be sustained by still more federal transfer payments as a source of personal income, and by choking free-market economic activity with further expansion of what George Will has called "the regulatory state."

So where can we find a handy roadmap marked with a route out of our current malaise and into a fast-changing future? Where, exactly, are the solutions? I'll give you, as I often do, an engineer's answer. To solve a problem, one first must define it as accurately as possible. Engineers know that some of the most spectacular structural failures are not buildings that collapse, but those that are constructed solidly but to no good end. Such a structure does not really address a need or solve a problem—leaving you with resources used up, no solution, and a solidly built public nuisance. Best to analyze any problem in tight focus, *then* take up detailed design issues.

That is why, if you think of this chapter as a movie, it brings just one element into focus: technological change. Everything else is intentionally blurred, or not even in the frame.

Government does have an important part to play in this movie, a larger role than merely keeping hands off enterprises and functions it should leave alone. The private sector provides our movie's producer, director, and even the stage on which the story unfolds. But technology hogs the storyline and rivets the attention of anyone with better vision than Mr. Magoo, the 1950s cartoon character whose near-sightedness was surpassed only by his inability to identify the problems he encountered. Globalization co-stars in this film—but a closer look reveals globalization deriving all of its depth, all of its drive, from technological change. One does not, after all, get one's tech support from Mumbai via snail mail. Educational reform and a new manufacturing paradigm comprise the movie's vital supporting cast, roles that raise the story beyond a fatalistic "and then, and then, and then." All other roles are bit parts. All subplots are mere distractions. Take the 2008 Great Recession as an example.

You might not lately have heard what happened in 2008 described as a "distraction." For most Americans the 2008 recession has not ended at this writing, four years after it began. If one accepts the statistical model's decree that the recession *has* ended, or is ending, then one enters the oxymoronic world of a jobless recovery, a concept central to our main concern here. Technology-driven efficiencies have been, and will continue to be, the main reason an economy can recover far faster than the unemployment rate. Those jobs are not lost to the impact of a financial crash; they are lost to the impact of new technology. Technological innovation is the flood tide we need to intercept and harness. Otherwise an endless recession will be followed by an endless depression. In such an event, financial events of 2008 will only have speeded the process a bit. Failure to seriously engage 21ˢᵗ Century technology will have been the cause.

In no way do I wish to diminish the impact of 2008's Great Recession. In fact, let me recap what a crushing series of events it has been.

If the Dallas Cowboys were "America's Team," for example, then home ownership was "America's 401K." Many generations of Americans believed that because a house was their biggest and most durable purchase, it was also their safest investment—one that would always rise in value. Today all those foreclosure notices dotting the landscape (in most cases representing families stripped of their nest egg) comprise the mere tip of the 2008 iceberg. Beneath the waterline one can find old people who haven't lost their home but who are unable to retire, or unable to move, because their home cannot be sold at a reasonable price, if at all. In many areas of the country one can choose a relatively new neighborhood and in a few minutes find younger people who bought a home in a short sale for a fraction of what it had sold for a few years earlier…but who are now themselves several feet underwater. Factor in damaged equity portfolios belonging to individuals or pension funds and this litany of hurt still barely outlines the scope of this "distraction."

If the 2008 crash had been a multi-car wreck along a busy highway, pity the poor traffic cop tasked with writing a report ascribing a percentage of blame to each driver. Amid the wreckage he would see bizarrely concocted financial derivatives that were bundled, sold, and sold again, then hedged against by the last party to the sale. He would see politicians and government and quasi-government agencies cheerleading for the sale of homes—new homes, large homes, *expensive* homes—to buyers who would never be able to make the payments. He would see home buyers who should have known better. He would see Wall Street entities that got out of the capitalization business and into the gambling business, sometimes betting against their own clients. He would be looking at anyone and anything, from individuals to governments, who grossly overleveraged his or its lifestyle, making "equity" a meaningless word. He would have to choose among so many causal agents for assigning a percentage of blame that he would run out of ink and paper while writing his report.

The misery index this mess left behind from coast to coast has not been equaled (except among families who sent sons and daughters to the battlefield) since the Great Depression. So how can I possibly call this, for purposes of our discussion, a mere *distraction*? Two reasons.

First, that now-familiar highlighted word: *irreversible*. It's difficult to imagine a better context, in fact, to ponder just how profound irreversibility is. Everything about the Great Recession, viewed as the consequence of financial lunacy, can be repaired. We might debate what went wrong and what needs to be repaired and how to repair it. But the carnage, painful as it is, is not permanent. It can be reversed, so long as we remain a great economic power on the world stage. The nature of financial crashes, in fact, explains why for at least four years pundits and ordinary people have been looking out the window waiting for "the recovery." Our economic engine historically has been so powerful that we have come to expect any financial disaster to self-repair, or something very near it. Call 2008 the most painful economic distraction most Americans now alive can remember, but unless we take the wrong path forward, it *will* be temporary.

Second, even if the tragic 2008 confluence of misfeasance and malfeasance and greed had not transpired, we would still have communities all across the land decimated by the loss of a major employer to another state or to another country or to the scrap heap of industrial evolution. Trusting in the status quo and in the end a gold watch for each employee, rather than diversifying even down at the level of a small town's economy, would have taken its grim toll—and will continue to do so. Absent 2008's economic nosedive, some towns would be less severely impacted, but would still be towns where "the plant isn't hiring like it used to." We would have that same depressed dynamic occurring in industrial pockets of our great cities. Even communities that are not struggling would be contributing to the aggregate millions of citizens who lack skills to find jobs, or to find jobs at a "living wage." Why? New technological efficiencies and globalization—a phenomenon all of us finally must stop wasting time demonizing, because globalization *is* irreversible. Competition rushes to fill every void of every business model, and 21st Century competition knows no borders.

Lashing out at global competition and globally connected economies is a futile thing, like a passenger trying to bail the Titanic with a teaspoon salvaged from the captain's table. Besides, unlike a sinking ship, there can be considerable upside to new technology—far more upside than downside. In fact, the simplest and perhaps most accurate way to define "our 21st Century problem" would not be "technological change," but "failure to embrace technological change in a smart way." This returns us to the four benchmark vectors. Technological change enabled the global economy. Education reform as a vital piece of the domestic employment picture is all about technology. Sustaining a manufacturing sector is all about

developing and applying new technology; the new manufacturing sector will be not just a producer of goods (and some
direct jobs), but a sort of laboratory annex that keeps our skills
as technology innovators from being lured offshore. That is a
tight circle for which technology serves as both circumference
and radius. The potential upside (and downside) of new 21st
Century technology dwarfs the economic "distraction" that
began in 2008. Technological change will be the dominant
ingredient of all foreseeable challenges and opportunities.

I have a friend, who despite being an engineering educa-
tor (a very good one), suggested in a conversation that perhaps technology was, *on balance*, a bad thing. Maybe, he
mused, all the destructive things human beings have done
with technology outweighed all the progress technology has
produced. This particular mind exercise is one I solved to my
own satisfaction long ago. I summed up for my friend just
the bare outlines of that progress, and asked in each case if
he would willingly revert to the "good old days." How about
life expectancy, I asked. We are living twice as long as humans did just a century ago. Would you give up that progress? "No." Improvement in our nutritional lives (even with
all the bad dietary choices millions make) can be illustrated
by the "they're bigger, stronger, faster" label put on modern-
era athletes. Would you give up that progress? "No." Our
pharmaceutical prowess accounts for the fact that no one now
alive has witnessed a fatal epidemic of medieval proportions.
Would you give that up? "No." We can travel in a few hours
to places it once took many months to reach. Would you give
that up? "No." We can communicate with each other from
any place on earth. Would you give that up? "No." The fact
is, many things that are irreversible—extraordinarily *important* things—are things we don't want to reverse.

Technology's power to determine economic and social history is so profound that one day it will require a whole new paradigm for defining the good life—meaning not just our prosperity, but what we *do* with our lives.   As long as I have been in the private sector I have wondered how society will respond when technology-driven efficiencies make "full employment" impossible in any traditional sense. Computers and machines and robots will never be able to do *everything*. Other factors—obviously including global competition—contribute to the fact that the world's foremost consumer nation employs fewer and fewer people to make the things it consumes. But there will come a day when a stunning and growing percentage of working-age Americans simply will not be needed to punch time clocks or draw salaries. The very word "job," I believe, will need redefinition.

I am not speaking as a utopian. Quite the opposite. I see the future's "unneeded" citizens—not because they lack skills, but simply because there is no traditional thing for them to do at any attainable skill level—as the ultimate foreseeable workforce problem. I really do. Speculating as to what percentage of the population the economy one day will no longer invite into "the shop" each day, and send a paycheck each week or month, cannot be done with any precision. I would guess half of Americans, at least. I would not be shocked if in some deep-future decade *more* than half of Americans will not be able to "find a job," as we now define how we spend our "workday." The human spirit was not designed for the couch potato life. We will need to do something about this. And, yes, I believe this "something" should still be driven by the private sector.

Dealing with, say, a 22nd Century 75 percent "unemployment rate" will be a genuine task for problem-solving in the very deep future. Right now we need to deal with unemployment and underemployment in the traditional sense, in a nation and era where high single-digit unemployment is unacceptable and where we should be putting millions more people to work. I believe this can be addressed, even as we look *far* ahead to a new paradigm for living a productive, contributing life (and having a financial livelihood) without a "job." Like agriculture a century ago, this future upheaval is mentioned here for just one reason: To illustrate that technology, not ideology, is the place to look for causal mechanisms and for *repair and replacement* mechanisms as we perform some needed maintenance on our old reliable engine of prosperity.

We need to become and remain firmly focused on the four parameters of current generations' interface with the 21st Century. We must avoid being distracted by old realities and old ideas.   This is not a time for debating whether unemployment compensation benefits should stretch into a third year for workers whose old jobs are gone forever. It is a time to assess how to convert technological change from a workplace liability to a workplace asset, and to revive the power of our economic engine. It can be done. Not addressing that task right now, if not sooner, is our biggest problem.

CHAPTER FOUR

Common sense, or bust

Even the very imaginative L. Frank Baum could not have imagined in 1900, when he published his tale about a wizard in a land named Oz, how his book would resonate throughout the century. Now, as the United States struggles to find traction in the 21ˢᵗ Century, we seem—like Dorothy's three Oz friends—to lack a heart, a brain, and courage. It's a do-or-die situation, so the courage issue is not whether we will act but whether we will act soon enough. The heart problem will be solved when we realize that going broke and becoming a second- or third-rate country is no route toward compassionate governance and widespread prosperity. Given courage and heart to advance as a society and as a nation, our very first steps *must* be smart. If we don't use our brain this show will close in Act One, regardless how much bravery and compassion we muster.

Forgive me for starting off, once again, with old 20ᵗʰ Century business. This time I'll avoid the ideology, barely touch politics, and focus rationally on issues that will be our 21ˢᵗ Century launch pad—or our Waterloo. Our sovereign debt, for example, now exceeds our GDP. Call that intersection the Stagnation Line, a functional and apolitical description. To view this index in action as sustained drama, take a look at Greece. Or for a larger but less flamboyant script, think back to the not at all distant past when Japan's star was in such ascendance that some feared Tokyo would buy up *all* of America's most coveted properties. Then Japan accepted a high debt-to-GDP ratio, and stagnation set in. No one worries these days about Japan buying and merging Disney, Coca-Cola, McDonald's, the NFL, and Yellowstone Park. Forget the politics. As a matter fact, can you even write a paragraph about Japanese politics? (Some of you can, I know; but you get my point.) Think of our challenge as setting off for a distant destination, but first having to move a fallen tree from the street right in front of your house.

Put 300 economists in a room for 150 days. Give them a podium, some audio/visual support, and half a day apiece to lecture about the Stagnation Line. Virtually all economists will say debt-to-GDP ratio matters, even in the United States. There will of course be bickering about exactly where the Stagnation Line occurs, whether the ratio matters more in one nation than another, various nuances of one kind or another, just how to quantify such parameters, and all the other data squabbling in which economists engage. One or two economists will scoff at any meaningful relationship between America's irrational sovereign debt and its economic recovery. For their trouble, they are likely to be awarded a Nobel Prize. Among the rest of us, common sense must prevail.

The Stagnation Line does matter. We need to break away from it, get our economic engine working again, and move into this new global technological age. Agreement on that need and that agenda appear to be exceeded only by total lack of action to answer the need and meet the challenge. Have you ever seen such a disconnect in public policy? I have not. It is an awesome thing. Three guys stand between two steel rails, which run in parallel along short wooden beams laid crosswise beneath the rails. A vibration along the rail system can be felt, an oncoming whistle can be heard from just up the line. The three fellows confer and agree they hear a railroad train, it is coming their way, and its arrival will prove fatal to anyone standing between these two steel rails. Yet the three do not move, and do not even *prepare* to move. What is wrong with this scene? Maybe, if strong consensus exists everywhere except among the 535 lawmakers who get to decide the issue, it's time for Washington *outsiders* (with a few sane insiders riding shotgun) to get this show on the road.

Intelligent, high-profile warnings about this train wreck have been available for years. Way back in 1992 (two decades is a long time these days), a truly bipartisan group called the Concord Coalition was formed to spread the gospel of fiscal sanity at the federal level. The Concord Coaltion has remained in business ever since, with membership over the years by serious people and serious entities—notably including former Senator Warren Rudman (a Republican), the late Senator Paul Tsongas (a Democrat), Pete Peterson (a successful entrepreneur and government adviser who has donated not only much of his life but a substantial amount of money to the cause), former Senator Bob Kerrey (a Democrat), the Brookings Institution, the Heritage Foundation, and David Walker (former comptroller general of the U.S.). The Concord Coalition in 2006 launched a national road show aptly dubbed the Fiscal Wake-Up Tour, appearing on college campuses and at electoral campaign events. But how many times have you seen the Concord Coalition represented on 24/7 broadcast news—even when the debt was being discussed? How many of your neighbors, as a result, even know that the Concord Coalition exists despite its 20 years of preaching education on our sovereign debt? When Rudman and Tsongas announced the coalition's formation just 20 years ago, by the way, our debt was barely one-fourth its current size.

The full and official name of the "debt commission" President Obama created in February 2010—now best known as "Simpson-Bowles" for the panel's bipartisan chairmen—was the National Commission on Fiscal Responsibility and Reform. The formal title makes sense. We certainly need both responsibility and reform. The commission came up with some reasonable (and genuinely bipartisan) proposals aimed at halting debt growth by 2014, then reducing the debt to 60 percent of GDP by 2023 and 40 percent by 2035. Our gridlocked political establishment not only ignored Simpson-Bowles, but sat and watched while $2 trillion was added to the debt in the two years after the panel was formed. A sad comment on Washington's inability to get anything done these days can be found by logging on to http://www.fiscalcommission.gov/ and clicking on "news." The moldy final item emanating from the panel, on January 31, 2011, bundled the members' individual comments on the report. Panel members themselves lacked enough consensus to make things happen. Not surprisingly, three-quarters of the commission members were sitting members of Congress.

Simpson-Bowles and the Concord Coalition have been beyond doubt the foremost players, among many, proselytizing on the need for budgetary sanity. The Simpson-Bowles panel even attracted some interest, however slight and shallow and ephemeral, from mass news media. Perhaps a "coalition to end all coalitions," featuring superstar academics and CEOs and retired statesmen, needs to convene itself, lean on news media for coverage and support, and shame our elected officials into action.

Whatever real or imagined body sets to work on the task (including, as a possible miracle, a Congress that comes to its senses), I would urge it to think and exhort beyond the "mere" matter of avoiding federal bankruptcy. No one can quarrel with that goal, of course. I agree entirely, even though I'm here to urge *new* spending (such as infrastructure) that genuinely promotes growth. But as well-taken as arguments about "balancing the federal checkbook" may be, I'd like to see this play out amid constant dialogue about fiscal integrity *and* spurring economic growth by "breaking away from the Stagnation Line." It would help a great deal, I believe, if everyone from ordinary citizens to policymakers to members of Congress grasped the dynamic of economic stagnation, its impact on the mantra of "Jobs! Jobs! Jobs!," and the fact that *this* is why federal budgetary integrity does matter. Keeping that foremost in mind might even help get something accomplished.

Like other contemporary centrists, I know what it means to feel lonely on matters of politics and policy. My thoughts about moving a near-bankrupt nation toward economic growth fit that pattern. Neither "balanced budgets at any cost" right-wingers nor "deficits don't matter" left-wingers can, in my view, get us out of this mess and onto a forward path. We need to sidestep both ideologies and robustly declare that private-sector economic growth is both the generator of American prosperity and the foundation of social equity. We need to follow that beacon as we forge a realistic budgetary policy. Any common-sense approach will include a certain amount of liturgy from both left and right, but at times must step on toes along either fringe. We need to put a stop/loss order on ballooning, unsustainable federal programs that will drive the United States ever deeper into insolvency. At the same time, we need to spend—and spend some more—in areas that will grow the economy rather than stunt it. We need to stop playing political games with promissory notes and unfunded liabilities.

We all, individuals and entities right up to and including the United States government, must operate within limits imposed by the realities of our resources and productivity. Greater resources and greater productivity mean fewer limitations. Fewer resources and stagnant productivity, or worse, mean fewer options, or none. That's what "you can take it to the bank" means. Our resources, assets, productivity, skills, prospects for growth, and positioning to survive a bad market or a new competitor or cruel weather (actual or figurative)...are what determine our lendability and, if you will, our "investability." If we put ourselves in a position to be blown away by the first strong wind, then we are like the person who says: "I wouldn't lend myself any money if I had it." The federal government seems hell-bent on proving that it will *always* be able to borrow money without consequence to the economy or the citizenry. That obviously is not true. For starters, there is the matter of what will happen when the cost of money rises above today's historic lows. Right now even the "cheap" interest on our sovereign debt equals annual growth in our GDP. That should scare anyone, except perhaps a terrorist who would like to blow us up without having to blow *himself* up.

You already know the truth of every word in the previous paragraph. Everyone does. That is why it can safely and fairly be called common sense. That same common sense must dictate our approach to reshaping government entities that have overrun present and future budgets. If we demonstrate serious discipline in that task, we will become a lendable entity and a rational borrower, a nation that is taking reasonable risks and upon which reasonable risks can be taken. That in turn will allow us to spend a few trillion dollars on vital infrastructure that has been ignored because of our fiscal mess. Having approached *that* in a disciplined way, with a real business plan for the future, we will become not merely lendable but investable. Then, and only then according to any bookkeeping I am familiar with, we will be positioned to enter the 21st Century. We will then be able to spend a *lot* of money in ways we must spend to grow the economy, which is our only path to survival. As a mere footnote, let me deploy the forgotten buzzword of a few years ago. This course of action will be the mother of all economic stimulus packages.

Perhaps the great disconnect that has prevented action on so many fronts is as simple as a mindless shout of "Hands off!" that seems to greet *any* reform effort involving any government entitlement program. Retirees and their surrogates, for example, routinely shout "Hands off my Social Security!" in response to reform proposals that will not affect their Social Security benefits in any way. This "Third Rail of American Politics" has a similar effect in Congress, where both political parties have at various times rejected change, or even discussion of change, as "dead on arrival"—except when the change will enhance benefits (and increase expenditures). Meanwhile, Medicare and Medicaid have joined Social Security as the great triumvirate of entitlements. Together, these three— two of which did not exist when I began working in the space program—account for almost half of today's federal budget. Older Americans live *decades* longer than when Social Security was created. By comparison, the workforce that pays retiree benefits is shrinking drastically. The demographics are so bad that if Social Security were a private insurance program, government regulators would shut it down. One need not possess even sixth-grade arithmetical skills to understand changes must be made.

In politics, though, "Hands off!" passes as sound policy,

especially when voiced by a reliable block of voters. Those same voters should give sober thought to how those same politicians pretend the Social Security Trust Fund contains money to pay future benefits. In fact, U.S. Treasury notes account for more than $2 trillion in the "trust fund." How nice it would be for any individual or a company that could raid its own rainy-day fund for $2 trillion, replace the cash with a $2-trillion IOU (or IOM, as in "I Owe Myself"), call the IOU an asset, take it to the bank and borrow more money—which is one way to cover nearly half of one's current expenditures.

Once again I find myself telling you things you already know. Once again common sense suffices to reveal both a call to action and a plan for action. Once again no action has been taken lately, and no one can be seen preparing for action on the near horizon. Once again I am not typing any late-breaking news here. But, as the chapter header suggests, the only alternative to heeding common sense, whether talking of entitlement programs or indeed our entire economy, is chaos and collapse. That seems worthy of note. For purposes of moving on and discussing the future, let's cross our fingers and assume leaders will be found and common sense will be heeded. Let's say the entitlement problem gets fixed, via whatever combination of deferred eligibility, means-testing, health-care reform, increased "contributions" (sounds so much better than "taxes")—all the usual proposals that have been kicked down the road for years. Let's assume that as a result one cannot foresee federal budgets being ever more consumed by these programs. Let's leave all that to common sense, leadership, and renewed national will. Then let's continue applying common sense to other vital programs with unaddressed pressing needs. Common sense, it seems, applies even to *21st* Century programs.

I said plural "programs" although public discourse al-

ways speaks of "infrastructure" as if it were a singular group-
ing, such as roads and bridges. Infrastructure in fact is many
things. Like the political center, the definition of infrastructure keeps adjusting itself in response to real-world needs.
One of Dwight Eisenhower's great achievements, perhaps
his definitive achievement as president, was creation of the
interstate highway system. Today all those eight-lane roads
are taken for granted. Few Americans driving today's cars
can remember when post-war Route 66 ran from "Chicago to
L.A., more than 2,000 miles all the way"—the vast majority
of those miles one lane in each direction. When Eisenhower
called for an interstate system to be constructed, it was a visionary leap forward. He knew such a system would give a
boost to the national economy, regional and local economies,
and would benefit all Americans.

We need similar vision today, even though our infrastructure looks much different. We still travel on countless mega-
tons of concrete. Propeller-engined airliners and land-line
telephones and file cabinets filled with paper, however, are
the stuff garage sales are made of. Those crumbling highway
bridges, many on the interstates—*are* a part of our serious
needs. But need also is reflected in the common complaint
heard from American travelers returning from some supposedly second-tier nation: "Their airports look better and work
better than ours." And there is more. We need to complete
our intent to bring every American address into the high-
speed digital wireless communications world, as the Post Office linked us all more than 200 years ago via real horses and
iron horses. At a time when fresh water is becoming precious,
crumbling water mains are wasting billions of gallons daily
(and ancient sewers are putting billions of gallons of waste
where it shouldn't be). I am sure a complete inventory of such

needs—and these are needs, not mere wants—would make the engineering society's infrastructure wish list look conservative. And I do not see any way of tackling these projects before brakes are applied, firmly, to 20th Century debt and entitlement issues. Do you?

Until this election season we barely heard a word from Washington about our infrastructure problem, other than an occasional and whimsical statement about projects that might get done someday, or a congressional hearing when a bridge collapses at rush hour—though it is true that the noise level can rise considerably when Congress *does* build a bridge that by common agreement goes to "nowhere." The prevailing silence might be wise from a politician's vantage point, given who is responsible for letting our nation's "*financial* infrastructure" fall into such disrepair. Washington, however, cannot hide this looming infrastructure crisis under a rock much longer. These projects must be tackled, they must be *paid for*, and they are far too costly to be added onto America's credit card while pretending our debt can be run up into infinity.

All government spending is linked in a holistic way that conveniently, for politicians, allows barrels of fiscal audacity to slip under radar. Many infrastructure projects, for example, are state and local projects. Grassroots governments are tax-powered entities but not sovereign nations. They cannot accrue sovereign debt and cannot print money. Most, in fact, are legislatively required to balance their budgets even as they pave streets, police the highways, house prisoners, pay for K-12 schools and public universities, license and regulate enterprises from salons to saloons, maintain local parks and recreation programs, promote tourism and agriculture—it's a very long list. This is not a small business. It is, in fact, an inverted pyramid. Local government employs about twice as many workers as state government, and state government employs about twice as many workers as the federal government.

No wonder, then, that state and local entities collect almost 40 percent of the nation's taxes (and, as a result of federal revenue-sharing, spend almost half of the country's total tax revenues). That is not a matter of federal magnanimity; it is a matter of Washington being empowered to tell state and local units what to do with their budgets. Medicaid, for example, is a major federal entitlement program. The states, however, historically have been mandated to pay about half the cost. Medicaid adds up to the biggest item in many state budgets. Nonetheless as far as the 24/7 broadcast and cyberspace news machine is concerned, government exists in just one place— Washington, D.C. Everything else is the minor leagues.

The people and the companies outside the Beltway know better because they write checks to states and counties and cities and townships to pay income and property taxes. They pay state as well as federal gasoline taxes. They pay state sales taxes. They pay FICA taxes to fund the big three entitlement programs, even if their wages are so low they pay no federal income tax. They have reached a point of low tolerance in these matters. Comparing America's federal taxes to some other nation's federal taxes is to compare apples and kumquats when numerous American states have larger GDPs, and budgets, than all but a handful of nations. Congress has become extraordinarily agile at passing costs on to local governments. But when Congress at last tackles "the infrastructure problem," there will not be much blood left to squeeze out of state and local turnips.

I think of a concerted effort to repair, upgrade and expand our infrastructure as being, in several ways, America's transition to the 21st Century. First, the infrastructure effort can't happen unless we successfully put the 20th Century's old business behind us. Second, none of the crucial issues we must address in the areas of technology and education reform and global interaction and smart manufacturing can be achieved without renewed infrastructure. Third, a certain spirit has been lost in this country, last seen in the national pride and achievement of the space program—which ironically led to many of the advanced materials that will be used in an infrastructure upgrade. Fourth, we desperately need to jumpstart the private economic growth engine that has been coughing and wheezing and coasting downhill for a dangerously long time. Do the first three and, in my opinion, the fourth will happen. Getting America in fiscal shape and of a national spirit to get on with these projects, and getting them well under way will be, in other words, the fulcrum that will leverage us into the new global technical era. Fitting, I think, to envision one of the six simple machines of the Renaissance—the lever—getting us off square one.

Let's not forget that this transition will be a genuine investment in things the entire spectrum of private enterprise can use to become more productive, and to move on into activities we will discuss in remaining chapters. Our society has accrued income inequities that cannot be sustained, no more than burgeoning entitlement and medical costs can be sustained. No closed-system, zero-sum, government-mandated scheme can solve either problem. In coming decades and onward only a reinvigorated, forward-thinking technology-driven private sector can do so, and only in a society where we restore, at all levels, a sustainable balance between that new economy and government spending.

If the United States were a company rather than the most important nation on earth, would an equity capitalist rate our company as the "most underperforming company on earth"? Are you kidding? Of course. America is grotesquely over-leveraged. Its business plan bleeds capital as far as the eye can see, at a quickening pace, with no credible effort in place to stanch the hemorrhaging. Meanwhile, it is producing new wealth at only a fraction of the rate it is spending. Any number of internal or global events could drive the cost of borrowing upward from its current historic lows. U.S.A. Inc. in its present directionless, insolvent, dispirited persona, would crash and burn.

Even before we complete the transition to the 21st Century, this fulcrum we might call the Infrastructure Program, in the national spirit we referred to the Space Program, can get the United States positioned to give the 20th Century a decent burial. Like the most solid restructuring plan ever seen in the corporate world, a U.S. government with a rational commitment to live within its means and a solid plan for *growing* those means, would not be just lendable and investable. It would at last and in actuality be doing what every politician promises—"moving forward again."

CHAPTER FIVE

We still need, very much,
that factory floor

No doubt it would be far more accurate these days to say "as American as *pizza* pie" rather than the traditional apple, given that the average American's slice consumption is now—what do you suppose—30...50...100 pizza slices for every wedge of apple pie? Mom's apple pie has become a casualty of, more than anything, the fact that Mom has left the kitchen to earn a paycheck. No offense to any ingredients in the iconic old Chevy commercial, but baseball is no longer our national pastime, hot dogs are under assault by nutritionists, few people put dessert pie of *any* kind in their daily regimen, and Chevrolet only recently has climbed back into a hard-fought wrestling match with Ford and Toyota for American nameplate supremacy.

Pie—presumably not pepperoni but the two-crust, fruit-filled type—nonetheless remains indispensable to any popular discussion of business, government, and the economy. Where would we be without pie charts? And, despite government's abysmal arithmetic in parceling out pieces of the pie, we all know that improving everyone's prosperity derives not from cutting bigger slices but from creating a bigger pie. That bigger pie hasn't been coming out of the oven lately. We need new improved ingredients and a new recipe. In addition, the process has been revised and the oven works in new ways.

Time now to adapt, or subsist on crumbs.

In the 1980s, as I grew JP Industries into a major auto components firm, new acquaintances usually asked me how big the company was. If I told them it was a half-a-billion-dollar company, they were likely to say: "No, I mean how many people do you employ?" That question no longer defines a company, and no one asks it anymore. For sure no one asks that question about General Motors, except in wonderment at how America has changed since the 1950s. But neither does anyone use workforce size to define new non-manufacturing icons such as Amazon or Facebook. Sales and profits determine the size of a company today. Some politicians and pundits have a quick, cynical, simplistic explanation for that new dynamic: corporate greed. They are wrong—wrong enough and populist enough to lead the gullible over the cliff we discussed earlier.

The nation's formerly largest corporation, for example, did not have a history of pushing workers out the door to maximize profits. The overly generous remuneration of the General Motors workforce, on the job and in retirement, was in fact one major cause of GM's financial catastrophe. Big government and big manufacturing *both* spent the last half of the 20th Century laying land mines beneath their own feet. How can one quarrel with that description of entities that wind up with retiree costs dwarfing current payrolls? It is complicated. Demographics of an aging population, efficiencies that require fewer and fewer employees to accomplish the same work, global competition driving down profit margins, that same competition leading to better products that last longer …it is an intricate picture. But unless one's mind is mired in a utopian, socialist fantasy, the bottom line is quite simple: compete or die. You can't make a bad product and sell it into a market of good products. And you can't sell a good product that costs twice as much as someone else's equally good product. This dynamic—a few outlier examples excepted, as with every endeavor under the sun—is not about greed. It is about centuries-old market truths, which are becoming even truer.

An eerie parallel to the GM saga can be found at the bottom of the government and taxation food chain, where numerous municipalities around the country have been lining up to declare bankruptcy or de facto bankruptcy. The only competition in the local government arena is with state and federal governments for tax dollars. At this most labor-intensive level of government, however, "legacy issues" are the same in a bankrupt city as in the old smokestack industries. Overly generous retirement and health-care benefits, padded payrolls, and slipshod fiscal management have left some cities struggling to pay retired workers even while current workers—including police officers—are being laid off. As a footnote to that fact, here—and in numerous other paragraphs of this book—I could easily add an exclamation point that asks: "Why did a thousand headlines proclaim that 'America Is Not Greece'?" Are you kidding? Show me a bankrupt American city and I will show you Greece without the Mediterranean.

In 1914, only 17 years before *Brave New World* was published, Henry Ford's assembly line workers were rejecting oppressive, mind-numbing production work in astounding numbers. Ford needed to hire and train more than three men if he wanted to find one who remained on the job at year's end. To solve this costly and counter-productive problem, Ford stunned the world by doubling workers' wages to five dollars. Ford's new pay scale famously increased number of consumers able to afford a car, but this was a mere footnote to his strategy. Ford's motive was to solve a productivity problem while keeping his product competitive. From a worker's vantage point it was all about a 100 percent pay increase (plus the bonus of an eight-hour workday instead of nine). From a business vantage point it was all about productivity (the eight-hour day meant Ford could operate three shifts a day, instead of two), getting those Model T's out onto Woodward Avenue, not wasting time spent hiring and training workers, and solving an acute labor shortage.

The automakers applied that template far past its rightful expiration date, into an era when labor costs were allowed to exceed common sense and management muffed a latter 20th Century challenge from foreign manufacturers. Almost 100 years passed from the $5 day until competition and technological realities and failure to live within their means brought the automotive American Three (formerly the Big Three) to their knees. In the real world, the sun rises and sets, death and taxes are certainties, and *any* business that doesn't compete will sooner or later—usually sooner—go bust.

During the manufacturing segment's American Century zenith, the platitude said that when Detroit sneezes, America catches a cold. That assertion might have been overused, but it was entirely true. Detroit was America's largest employer. Its indirect economic impact defied calculation. The steel industry, parts manufacturers, electronics and glass companies, road builders, garage mechanics, salesmen—even a huge part of the advertising and newspaper and broadcasting businesses—stayed healthy only if Detroit stayed healthy. That was no mere sneeze you heard at the dawn of the 21st Century. The bigger they are, the harder they fall.

Detroit's car companies, made vulnerable by complacency and after staggering for several decades, nearly went down for the count. Those humiliating few weeks on the brink might be the place to mark the true beginning of the 21st Century. Historians could find few bookends more aptly symbolic than the $5 Day on one end and The Bailout on the other. All four 21st Century benchmark vectors played a role in the latter bookend—global competition, technological advances (the first widespread, heavy-duty, real-world use of the word "robot" occurred in the car industry), the need for education reform (no Henry Ford waits at today's factory door to hire and train, at double pay, workers straight off the farm or straight off the boat), and a synergistic need for new thinking in our manufacturing segment (for direct job creation, of course; but equally important as a nearby laboratory to continue our status as an exporter of innovation). It all added up to that very 21st Century matter of Vector One companies becoming a source of unemployment rather than a source of new jobs.

Perhaps no image so perfectly signaled the futility of resistance to the coming new century as did those photos of angry American autoworkers taking sledgehammers to Japanese-made cars, even as the Japanese were moving to build cars in America (competitive cost and productivity realities, you know). The days of bludgeoned Toyotas are past, but more sophisticated (and more dangerous) resistance to the new era remains. We need to do more than merely accept that the calendar has turned; in a single grasp, we need to confront the new century and embrace it.

One can forgive the politicians and the pundits and the unemployed themselves for chanting "Jobs! Jobs! Jobs!" That is after all a noble and very American chant, quite different than "Handouts! Handouts! Handouts!" The trick will be to move the dialogue (and the chants) away from instant (and obsolete) jobs, while avoiding surrender to the handout mentality. Instead, we need to chant for a new job-creating environment and a new paradigm for producing qualified job candidates. There *was* a time when it might have been valid in a recession to expect jobs could materialize from a tweaked tax rate here, a money-supply adjustment there, or—mostly, like a fresh breeze inevitably closes out a heat wave—an "uptick in the business cycle." That always happened sooner or later after Detroit caught a cold. Today's challenge is not cyclical. It is fundamental and technological. No one would have accomplished much by standing in a 1912 cornfield chanting: "Farm jobs! Farm jobs! Farm jobs!"

The farm-to-factory social and technological upheaval, though massive, was a small reflection of where we stand today. No one has constructed an oven the size of Kansas in which to bake a much, much larger Mom's apple pie. If we are smart, we'll make manufacturing the core—and "core" is precisely the right, if surprising, word—of how we meet and mold the future. We can make the American manufacturing sector our prime route toward "Jobs! Jobs! Jobs!" once again …not as directly as in the past, not in any 20th Century way, but nonetheless as a vital driver of prosperity for all. Millions of lunch buckets won't be carried into the factories of the future. The livelihood of most Americans, however, will depend on the health of American manufacturing.

As we talk about bringing our manufacturing sector into a new era, we need to keep a couple things in mind about this powerhouse that drove the American Century. More than 70 years have passed since FDR, a year before Pearl Harbor, dubbed our mills and factories "The Arsenal of Democracy." It has been a long time since you heard commonly expressed awe about our "industrial might." The numbers, however, remain mighty.

First, the service sector (and especially computer-related

technology) has radiated all the workplace sex appeal for a generation or two, but guess what? We remain the world's largest manufacturer. In 2011 we produced a fifth of the entire world's manufacturing output. If one must pick oneself up after being knocked down, that is the best possible floor to start from.

Second, it is true that manufacturing accounted for 31 percent of U.S. non-farm employment in 1950 and that 60 years later that percentage had dipped below 10 percent, but guess what? Almost 12 million Americans work in today's manufacturing sector, a number that posted modest gains in 2010 and again in 2011—the first years that had seen an increase since 1997.

Third, 12 million jobs is a lot of jobs, no matter what percentage they might be of our total workforce. Despite its troubles, U.S. manufacturing obviously has not been driven into antique status by an inability to compete. It is nowhere near extinction. It has so many assets, in physical plant and productivity and business culture, that if we did everything wrong and stayed on the road to government-centric and dwindling world importance, we would *still* be making things. Not enough things. Not the right things. Our people would suffer from all that dwindling. But we would remain on the list of manufacturing countries. Take just one-half of our current *manufacturing might* and set it down in any other leading developed country and you would be looking at the new global superpower.

In other words, American manufacturing has big challenges today, and faces bigger challenges tomorrow, but is nowhere near being a disaster zone. Viewed as a single unit in a mind exercise, one could analyze the U.S. manufacturing sector as a single underperforming company—one with an upside and a downside the likes of which have never been seen in world history.

The downside would be to let a vibrant, highly productive, innovative conglomerate atrophy quickly into mediocrity with dangerous consequences for all Americans. The upside would be to refocus the world's largest, most important "company" in midstride, nip its foreseeable problems in the bud, retool (as all manufacturers do), and soar to new heights as the winner and still champion of a larger, well...*global pie*. The bad news is that American manufacturing has reached a decisive crossroads. The good news is that the proper path to choose is obvious. The further bad news is that American society (meaning all levels of government and the will of the people) must commit to the live-or-die effort (see "infrastructure," see "education"). The further good news is this manufacturing re-birth *can* be achieved, if we somehow summon that shared re-solve—which seems to be the key to success when one looks at these 21st Century survival issues from any direction.

No one could estimate with acceptable accuracy how many Americans would be willing (or fiscally able) to report to work at the wage rates foreign suppliers pay offshore work-ers to produce countless low-value products. My best guess is almost none would sign up. Americans already turn their back on jobs paying wages that, although low by our standards, are much higher than millions of manufacturing jobs around the world. If someone in Asia produces wood screws that could be made here by workers earning less than half the U.S. mini-mum wage—is that a question worth asking? Should we even bother bemoaning the loss of such jobs? Of course not.

Nor could anyone estimate with acceptable accuracy the number of American manufacturing jobs that have been lost as a direct result of companies moving overseas, or as a direct result of imported goods taking market share from domestic

product, or as a direct result of domestic regulatory and taxation issues, or as a direct result of new efficiencies. Technological advances would have eliminated a significant number
of jobs from the factory floor even if no factory existed anywhere in the world except the lower 48 states. That fact is
among the reasons it's impossible to sort out reasons jobs are
exported, let alone add up accurate numbers.

Let's imagine a hypothetical small-town Midwest plant
where 2,000 employees manufacture dishwashers. Let's say
that one sad morning the entire operation disappears to Mexico, where workers are paid a small fraction of Midwestern
wages. The reason for the exodus appears cut-and-dried: pay
rates. But there are also regulatory issues, including some
that do not involve worker safety or sensible stewardship of
natural resources. There are tax issues (the dishwasher company has been marginally profitable, at best, for 15 years, but
in each of those years it has paid 30 percent of the town's
school system budget, bought all its police cars, and paid a far
larger share of water and sewage costs than pro rata accounting would demand). The plant's union has accepted a pay
freeze in several contract negotiations—but refuses to budge
on antiquated work rules (antiquated, of course, by new technology), and actively nurtures workforce resentment against
management. While the plant's profitability slouched toward
ancient history, two of its major suppliers outsourced key
parts to...Mexico. For these and other reasons—bottom line
being compete or die—there is *no way* this plant could stay
in the Midwestern town where it had been an icon for many,
many years.

Keeping in mind that technological advances are irreversible, and that a light breeze of new technology can produce
gale-force change in a given market, "tech" clearly is short-

hand for both the problems and the solutions we are discussing. Technology's long-term impact upon the job market, in
fact, dwarfs all the headline-grabbing events that first created
a new meaning for an adjective (offshore), then a brand-new
verb: "to offshore, as in 'Ajax offshored its parts department.'"

Technological advances even played a major role in the
loss of our mythical dishwasher factory to Mexico, though
that might not be apparent. Communications technology and
transportation technology, for example, today allow a product
to be assembled and shipped in containers from the farthest
village on the planet. A warehouse supervisor in Brooklyn (or
anywhere else) can tell you in an instant the exact location of
a particular unit still in its crate—the kind of tracking that not
many years ago would have required time and effort even if
that particular dishwasher were sitting in the warehouse a short
walk from the supervisor's desk. Inventory management, the
parts pipeline, quality control—a very long list of chores have
been simplified and improved by technology that already has
begun to seem old, and which makes offshoring a competitive
solution in situations where it used to be impossible.

Meanwhile, when dishwashers—and numerous other
home appliances—arrived on the consumer scene they were
met with acclaim befitting futuristic technological marvels.
But one by one, as their technology became commonplace (as
did their mass manufacture), these appliances morphed into
mere manufactured *commodities*. That is, unless they are built
by a truly inept company, all models in the same price range
are essentially the same in construction and quality no matter
who builds them. I would argue—and have so argued—that
even today's automobile, the mass-marketed models at least,
have become manufactured commodities. If one buys any
major carmaker's best-selling mid-sized sedan with similar

amenities, one can expect to get a good product that will run well, last a long time—and carry the same number of people, at the same speed, in the same comfort, with approximately the same gas mileage and safety as any other best-selling mid-sized sedan. You will of course quarrel with that assertion and defend your favorite brand, for various idiosyncratic reasons. In some subjective ways you may be right...just a little bit. But a well-constructed car of a particular class is a well-constructed car of a particular class. Much like, say, dishwashers of a particular size and class.

Any of these durable goods products is infinitely more sophisticated and differentiated than a generic bushel of wheat or a silver ingot, for sure. A side by side refrigerator is a manufactured commodity, not a raw product. But the days when Frigidaire was synonymous with refrigerator (or Kodak synonymous with camera) are long gone. The things that most endear a particular automotive nameplate to buyers these days are cost and service—two things that cannot be manufactured into a product. The cost factor is decided in the engineering and design departments before manufacture begins. Superlative service is something the customer receives after the product has been designed, manufactured, shipped, and sold. Absolutely nothing about these two crucial factors has a thing to do with whether the product is made in Illinois or the other side of the world.

So it's a wide range of manufacturing that has been, or threatens to be, shoved offshore by competitive forces. Some products—*many* products—offer no reason whatsoever for trying to keep their manufacture in the U.S. No one here wants to work making, say, Polynesian cocktail umbrellas at 25 cents an hour. We lose no technological edge by letting someone else, somewhere else, do that work. Goodbye,

Mai Tai swizzle stick manufacturing. Gone for good. That's easy (and intentionally simplistic). But what about those dishwashing machines? What about, say, the American furniture and textile industries, which have seen historic local economic bases pack up and leave northern locales, relocate in the southern U.S., then move yet again, this time offshore? We'll leave parts of those valid questions to be answered in later discussion of globalization. Here, let's stipulate three things—irreversible change is irreversible, free markets are not merely a good thing but the *only* way to grow that economic pie, and "compete or die" is an absolute. If we honestly acknowledge those three things (and we have no other choice), then any forward-looking discussion about 21st Century manufacturing— painful as it may be for workers who made those dishwashers and textiles and furniture—is not at all difficult to outline.

First, the profit centers in manufacturing (and therefore the best and best-*paying* jobs) involve deploying the latest technology to produce value-added goods. You can use dayglow paint and the best wood available in the Far East, but you simply are never going to add any value to those cocktail umbrellas. They are what they are, toothpicks and paper, a very bottom-tier commodity. Building a contemporary midsized automobile, on the other hand, is not a matter of dropping an engine on a chassis and adding some fenders, which more or less is what happened on the Model T's horseless carriage assembly line. Today's car is a manufactured commodity, but it also is a mobile technology center of magnificent scope—loaded with on-board computers and high-precision mechanical components, engineered for safety and reliability that would stun those who designed any of America's classic cars. Making cars is one kind of manufacturing we want to keep in the United States. Fundamental to understanding

21st Century manufacturing, however, remember that it takes fewer workers to *assemble* one of these modern marvels than it took to assemble a Model T. No doubt it will take even fewer workers in the future than it does now—as I discussed in that old Grand Rapids speech.

Second, *any* manufacturing that uses high levels of new technology is the kind of manufacturing we want to keep on these shores. That's true even if its labor force is small, even if its direct contribution to GDP is so tiny as to not show up on economic radar. Why do we care about such a company? A tiny, technology-intensive company surely means nothing to the economy in the way a car manufacturer's payroll does. Absolutely true; a GM job roster is a precious thing to be treasured, even if it is but a shadow of its old self and even as it shrinks because of new efficiencies. But it isn't workforce size that makes the car companies—*plus* any companies that demand new technology but amount to mere blips in the economy, *plus* all other technology-consuming companies of any intermediary size—the core of our 21st Century economic paradigm. Almost all these companies, just like 19th or 20th Century companies, will continue to demand varying degrees of raw materials and finished parts, require vendors of every type, and hire their share of accountants and sales reps, and plant maintenance people—every job description imaginable. What makes these companies uniquely vital to the 21st Century, though, is not their direct employment, but all that technology consumption. That's because . . .

Third, technology—rather than the durable goods our manufacturers produce—could fairly be viewed our most important *product* in the 21st Century. It's a close-knit synergy. For example:

• Technology, as noted, fuels the most prosperous manufacturing industries, which are excellent creators of new wealth, the lifeblood of any vibrant, growing, free-market economy.

• It logically follows—and experience usually supports the logic—that high-tech manufacturing wants its best sources of new technology to be located nearby. A sophisticated manufacturing facility that winds up thousands of miles from its laboratory will, if possible, tend to move the lab near its manufacturing facilities. Similarly, an industry that has its labs and all the best related outside intellectual support based in the United States has, obviously, a good reason to "stay home."

• New technology derives from both private and public research, sometimes jointly and sometimes singly, but in either case demanding a world-class university system.

• The United States currently boasts the foremost graduate schools on the planet, as evidenced by the world sending so many of its best and brightest here for an American education. One could compile a long manifest of reasons we should sustain this technological/educational leadership. For reasons apparent within this book's context, we *must* maintain that leadership.

• The concept of technology as a "product" is not really a figurative thing. Technology is intellectual property. It makes things work. Once a product's ingredients advance beyond raw materials and sweat and toil, it is technology that adds value to that product. The right technology in the right application is a profitable thing. Companies buy and sell technology every day. Occasionally a nefarious company (more often a nation) will steal technology, or will produce a quasi-legal clone of a technological process. Technology is real, as solid as the chair you are sitting in.

• A new piece of technology—in its pure conceptual form,

or as a plan for application in manufacturing, or as a completed high-tech manufactured product…or in the nascent form of a new Ph.D.'s brainpower—will be our greatest 21st Century *export*. Again, it *must* be thus, or this is most definitely not going to be a great century for the U.S.

That is "smart manufacturing," one of our four benchmark vectors. We must manufacture value-added products that consume new technology. To do that we must create the new technology our manufacturing sector needs. Then we need to train, endlessly, a manufacturing workforce that can get the job done. And along the way we need to make smart choices about plugging this new "manufacturing might" into global markets. It's a spectacular synergy. But I think you can see why even though it's "all about technology," it's also all about a new 21st Century manufacturing sector.

"Jobs! Jobs! Jobs!"? Yes indeed. But not in any 20th Century form. Before too long, in fact, millions of jobs will exist that none of us today can describe, anymore than Columbus could describe, accurately, where his little ships were headed. That same unpredictability could be said of entire as-yet unborn industries. Who can predict the precise layout of a high-tech manufacturing matrix derived from new technology several generations into our future, when we don't yet have a handle on new technology's impact this afternoon? This is not a time for planning instant obsolescence with short-sighted, laborious, bureaucratic, *faux* precision. The proper path is obvious, but is not marked by GPS coordinates. It is indeed, as those old guys said on the shop floor decades ago, "all about the United States continuing to make things." Our universities and those free-market manufacturers who perform best can get us to our destination, but only if the politicians—and a lack of public will—don't mess things up.

CHAPTER SIX

If it's all about technology, it's all about education

The world is a better place because of great novelists and poets and painters and musicians and sculptors and actors. We could include great chefs on a short list of specialists who add value to our cultural lives. Even such a basic need as food, after all, can be lifted above the ordinary and into the realm of art. As a voracious consumer of the arts (and occasional patron of the arts), and as someone who enjoys a wonderfully prepared meal, I obviously believe esthetic marvels enrich us all. I also believe *everyone's* education should include a well-guided tour of the literary, visual, and musical arts. But only a relative handful of citizens can pay the rent by knowing the difference between a sonata and a fugue, or by sharing their opinion of *Moby Dick*—or, for that matter, by knowing how to play a fugue or write a novel or choose the best fresh ingredients and bring them to table well enough to rent a building and start printing menus. The world doesn't work that way. The overwhelming majority of us always have needed to make a living in the mundane realm of commerce and industry (or, via subsidy by the private sector, government). Education's role in that familiar dynamic must be fundamentally recast, however, for the 21st Century.

At a glance, educating young people for the 20th Century workforce didn't look much different than what education must accomplish in the new age. For example, all young people preparing for today's job market know the fashionable acronym "STEM," meaning "science, technology, engineering, and math." Pointing toward a STEM career means, according to a 2011 Bureau of Labor Statistics essay, preparing for a job that will...

"...play an instrumental role in expanding scientific frontiers, developing new products, and generating technological progress. These occupations are concentrated in cutting-edge industries such as computer systems design,   scientific   research and development, and high-tech manufacturing industries. Although educational requirements vary, most of these occupations require a bachelor's degree or higher. Accordingly, STEM occupations are high-paying occupations, with most having mean wages significantly above the U.S. average."

That BLS quote is entirely true this afternoon, and was entirely true decades ago (*many* decades ago, if you eliminate reference to computers). College graduates now in their 70s and older understood, back in their own school days, a marketplace distinction between a degree in "hard science" and a "soft" degree. If you possessed the inclination and grit and aptitude to follow the former path, toward being not a poet but a lab rat, you were more likely to be rewarded with "job security" and a larger paycheck. So that part of the new acronym isn't really news. In 1940 parents would rather foresee their sons (and now, increasingly, daughters) as engineers or scientists or medical doctors than as shoe salespersons or postal workers or even "schoolteachers." That is not to demean the other occupations. Parental preference for a hard-science education over an arts or literature degree, and certainly over jobs requiring only a high-school degree, did not derive from a love of calculus or biology. It came straight from the near-universal desire to see one's offspring thrive and lead a prosperous life. The hard sciences were never a poor path to that result, especially in a parent's mind's-eye. An offspring who became an engineer or a researcher or an M.D. with a bent for the arts could always, after all, afford a grand piano and season tickets to the opera.

What has changed about that dynamic, and continues to change at an increasing pace, is basically threefold and could be summarized as "it's more true than ever." First, more and more jobs—not merely those in the "STEM career" path—require a certain level of math and science literacy, and almost any career requires or is at least enhanced by advanced computer literacy. Second, as countless studies and simple observation reveal, a larger and larger percentage of available jobs will require bachelor's and advanced degrees in math and science and engineering. Third, whether you are a Ph.D. doing pure research, or a community college night student making car components by day in a Midwest factory, you will need appropriate *continuing* education as surely as a surgeon or psychologist. Keeping one's skills in sync with evolving technology means shooting at not just a moving target but an accelerating target. Profound changes in the workplace will become more profound. The need for parallel changes in how we prepare employable workers and keep them employable is obvious.

The workplace is market-driven. Competition creates profound change without any prompting by new government policies or regulations, without any kibitzing other than what the marketplace has to say. Any new manufacturing technology, any more efficient process becomes a prerequisite for survival. Large workplaces that don't heed free-market cues to change will go under—or send their CEOs to Washington, hat in hand, to seek rescue via unorthodox, taxpayer-funded bankruptcy. Industries that can infect an entire economy just by sneezing might find relief that way (though their secured creditors will not). But even in the case of GM and Chrysler's bailout, the result was massive change. GM, in fact, became almost unrecognizable. Necessary fundamental change in the workplace can happen only if our educational system heeds three *new* R's: reform, refocusing, and response.

I am not here to suggest exactly *how* our K-12 schools can best be reformed to produce students who are better readers, better at math, more devoted to scientific method, and more literate in those cultural enrichments mentioned at the outset of this chapter …to say nothing of making a better impression at job interviews. The experts will need to find answers within a daunting environment that includes new family dynamics, social change, instant and omnipresent communications media, and budget constraints. Such answers, however, must be found. We are the world's greatest nation and yet we have communities in which most kids do not graduate from high school, and many of those who do graduate lack any credible readiness for further education. Schools in almost every district are engaged in a running battle with a standardized testing system that may or may not be adding value to the educational process. The American public school system, including its urban schools, once could claim a gold medal for democratic excellence. Today, among parents, some of the loudest educational buzz is about "charter" schools as a means of avoiding these same public schools. Too many schools are failing both as educational institutions and as centers of socialization and security. It will take some of the best minds of this generation, fully dedicated to the problem, to find solutions and instill public confidence.

Meanwhile, every graduation day, for better or worse,

millions of our offspring take one more step—we hope—toward entering a fundamentally changed, and changing, workforce. In that regard I *am* here to suggest that our schools, however they attack their demons from the bottom up, must pay more attention to the workplace. It's true that schools are tasked with preparing students for a life, not just a work life. I remain fervently in favor of providing that guided tour of the arts for everyone, and I do not believe eighth-graders need to be or should be deciding whether they will become surgeons or teachers or ironworkers. But precious few students will find life rewarding without ability to compete—first for a job and then within a workplace culture, or as an entrepreneur. Jobs that require only a high-school education while offering new employees a career that will support a family are virtually extinct. A good salesperson can always make a good living, of course—sometimes a very good living. But any young person with that path in mind should interview a few sales managers and find out how many newbies must be hired and fired before a single success story is written. There is no avoiding the fact that every 21ˢᵗ Century K-12 student needs to be exposed to as much "STEM" education he or she is capable of completing successfully.

Exceptions to the STEM advantage tend to be entrepreneurial, unless you are that 1-in-20 salesman or that 1-in-20,000 athlete or 1-in-50,000 artist or musician. (Excuse my wildly unscientific estimates.) Some exceptions are, of course, as enormous as it can get. Bill Gates is often, and accurately, described as the world's richest college dropout. Gates is not the only entrepreneur who became wealthy without a college degree. Almost every town in America includes *high-school* dropouts on its roster of serious entrepreneurial success stories. Behind every statistic, including the BLS numbers regarding the workforce outlook for those trained in science and technology, lurks someone who has shattered that statistic's expectations. Unfortunately, the someone who did the shattering did it on his or her behalf alone, not for others in the statistical group. Outliers—positive or negative—are mere blips in the statistics. Many people live to defy the life insurance industry's actuarial tables, but the tables nonetheless are bankable. Do not quarrel with numbers that say the more science and technology you have in your educational resumè, the better off you will be in the job market. The numbers are indisputable even if you know someone with a Ph.D. in physics who is living in his parents' basement and working as a night-shift manager in the fast-food sector.

There you have a few words about the first two 21st Century "R's" in our education dilemma, one bearishly difficult and one incredibly obvious. The first, a bearishly difficult question about *reform* (which of course I leave to the experts to answer), is: What must our educational establishment do to confront an era in which external social factors have helped diminish the quality of our K-12 output, even as career paths are demanding better-prepared high-school graduates? The second, incredibly obvious puzzle piece is this *refocus*: No offense to the "soft" or liberal-arts faculty and curriculum, but what today's students will most *need* as adults is every successful hour of science and technological education they and the system can handle. With a little will to act, this second element is simple (in concept, a least), nothing more than a bit of a shift in emphasis, and an intense effort to make science and technology education absolutely as inclusive as possible. Throughout his or her K-12 education, no capable student should be allowed to make a soft landing away from fundamental science studies. It's as obvious as the statistics about

STEM graduates. It becomes much more obvious if one simply looks around to see a citizenry that is literally plugged into technology most of their waking hours.

That leaves a third "R"—*response*. This element is all about change, and relates to education as FedEx and UPS relate to the Pony Express.   "Exponential change" has been a popular phrase for a generation or two. In the scientific sense of the word, *exponential* change means change of a magnitude equal to a mathematical exponent, those superscript numbers in an equation. In other words, a particular exponential change would upset the proverbial apple cart to the second or third or fourth or 50th power—or as is also popularly, and without specificity, used in daily conversation, "to the *nth* degree." Despite all the common usage of such phrases, and despite my talk about *fundamental* change, it is important here to note that for the most part I am not talking about the need for our educational system to deal with "exponential change." If the exponent were merely modestly large and quick, it would be an impossible task. We haven't reached that point, at least not yet.

Technology does advance with remarkable speed, sometimes with breathtaking speed, occasionally with stunning speed. We have come to expect that technology will make fundamental changes in the world within a single lifetime. But we do not wake up on Monday and find the printing press invented, wake up on Tuesday to discovery of the microprocessor, arise on Wednesday to find the first personal computer being marketed, greet Thursday with our first peek at the internet, and end the week attending a dedication for the first advanced manufacturing plant that does not employ a single human being, not even a security guard. Calculate an exponent spanning each of those morning surprises, if you wish. But console yourself, as an education reform planner, in knowing that a 21st Century education system must move merely very, very fast…not impossibly fast.

It's also important to note that despite my interest as a citizen in K-12 education, this book is essentially about how, as the politicians *always* (meaning something that never changes, exponentially or otherwise) say, getting the country moving again. That means growing the economy, in a free-market setting, so as to create a larger pie and thus benefit everyone who participates in the process. And although better grade-school outcomes and better high-school outcomes absolutely will help in that effort, it is at the college and university levels where the fastest, most direct connection occurs. That is the only connectivity level with which I have had direct experience as a technology manager and entrepreneur. It is the only connectivity level where education can seek to move if not quite as rapidly as technology moves, then at least respond rapidly enough to nurture a competitive workforce and continue to produce a domestic "technology supply" that has fast become the world's most valuable raw material.

In other words, when our colleges and universities offer curricula that turn on a dime to support the changing technological savvy required of world-class manufacturing employees, then our manufacturers will know their workforce can compete globally for the long term. And if our colleges and universities continue to produce graduates who create world-class technology, either in academic research or in the private sector…then our great holistic economic engine, if allowed to run at full speed, will remain unchallenged as the world's foremost sustainable generator of per-capita prosperity. World-class research and scientific education have been our strong suit for a very long time, and remain ours to sustain or lose. The quick-turnaround "continuing education" of the

workforce, top to bottom, is the new, 21st Century TECHNOL-
OGY IMPERATIVE.

Just-in-time manufacturing came on the scene as a managerial strategy that increased efficiency, reduced inventories,
aided quality control, reduced costs, and enhanced profits. It
is tempting, and I think valid in a certain sense, to think here
of "just-in-time technological education" for the manufacturing sector. Similar to a new part being manufactured just in
time to keep an assembly line moving efficiently, a college can
create a new training class—whether an actual, semester-long
course with hourly credits, or simply a seminar unique to a
particular company—that will bring workers up to speed on a
brand-new piece of technology. Unlike just-in-time manufacturing, however, it's not a matter of delaying the process until
the *last* effective moment; "just-in-time education" is about
providing knowledge at the *first* practical moment in the face
of rapidly advancing technology. In either case, something
happens just in time. With parts and inventory it's a matter of
being just in time, on the back side, for efficiency and profit.
In the educational arena it's a matter of being just in time, on
the front side, for *survival*. A workforce that falls behind the
educational curve is a workforce that might soon be without
a workplace because others are moving quicker to integrate
new technology. It can happen not just to one plant, but to an
entire market sector.

When JP Industries began operations in 1979, I walked
straight into the world of acquiring manufacturing companies
that could and should be doing better, improving their operations, and integrating each new unit as a synergistic piece of
the larger corporate entity. This is equity capitalism. I did not
invent the process, but I was an early student of the process
and soon thereafter a practitioner. Contrary to equity capital's

poor image in some quarters as a mere "bleeder" of companies that otherwise would have thrived, most such acquisitions—and every acquisition I was involved with—pursue the long-term best business plan and operational strategy for any acquired unit. A hypothetical 200-employee company that survives and thrives for the foreseeable future as a 150-person company, for example, has emerged in a better position than an obsolescent 200-employee company that would have clunked along for a year or two or three, then gone out of business. The numbers are different with every acquisition, and the possible parameters are infinite. But that is the model I followed throughout my entrepreneurial career.

Some acquisitions are more successful than others. Usually there is a near-instant reduction in payroll. One could say "of course" that's true, because in most cases the plant was for sale because it was bloated or otherwise inefficient. Often the owner could not solve its problems and did not see a good future for it. In some cases lost jobs eventually returned in part or in whole after efficiencies and new technology were implemented. This entire era of American manufacturing, don't forget, did not occur in the same environment as, say, the Eisenhower era. In the middle of the 20th Century many undeveloped nations would have been hard-pressed to produce even those aforementioned cocktail-stirring umbrellas. Most of Europe's great factories had been bombed into rubble. Japan was just beginning to reinvent its manufacturing base. The cargo container had not been invented. It was assumed that except for specialty items and products we did not wish to make, we owned the manufacturing trading lanes, and that most of what arrived here from the Orient was junk. You know how that story turned out.

Within a few decades, manufactured goods and components of every stripe, from cars to TV sets, were flowing in this direction. Small and medium-sized companies across the heartland could no longer coast along with marginal efficiency, barely caring about new technology, and sending the sales force out twice a year for a seasonal handshake. Many, however, remained stuck in the old culture. That was the operational environment in which equity capitalists came on the scene to triage underperforming companies, creating a healthy new life for many, almost always with a regimen that included dead-weight loss. It is fair to say that my company and others were not always the most popular arrivals in town. It is also fair to say that an underperforming and troubled company's prospects are seldom a secret, so our arrival was welcomed, though rarely cheered, more often than you might think. At any rate, JPI never overleveraged a deal, and never bought a company for no reason but to sell its component parts for a quick profit. I selected underperforming companies which, if brought up to their potential for efficiency and quality, could contribute to our corporation and stay around for a long time. That was not merely an honorable way of doing business; it was vital to the economy—and will remain so.

One such acquisition was a small manufacturing operation in Grand Haven, Michigan, where several hundred employees made automotive camshafts. That product was a good fit for JPI. It came as no surprise to anyone when one of our first actions was to lay off perhaps 15 percent of the workforce, the first step toward bringing the operation into a reasonable state of competitive efficiency. Soon thereafter we saw a way the plant could produce better, more competitive, more profitable camshafts by transferring newer technology to the operation. The technology was already in use by a JPI unit in Germany. Some of our German employees flew to the shores of Lake

Michigan and led any necessary retraining of our Grand Haven technicians and machinists. The new technology brought in more orders—meaning a workforce that previously had to be shrunk for efficiency's sake was hiring new employees *because of* technological efficiencies.

At another plant, in western Iowa, workers began feeling out the new ownership—us—to see what they could do to improve their own prosperity. Some of their proposals, particularly on benefits that these days are called "legacy issues," simply would not work within the plant's bottom line. Recent, and ongoing, debacles involving both government and private-sector legacy costs show what can happen when you promise the moon at midday. When JPI explained this to the Iowa workers, some employees raised the idea of profit-sharing. I suggested that could be a fine idea, as long as productivity remained high and as long as there were profits to share. We moved toward a plan that seemed like a win-win situation until we hit a surprise stumbling block. It became clear that many employees, perhaps most, had no idea how to read a balance sheet. Some could not differentiate revenue from profit. What to do? A call from JPI to the local community college resulted in creation of a brief "course," just for us, on how to read financial statements. Suddenly the workers had a profit-sharing program, understood it, knew how to communicate about it, and in most cases developed a heightened interest in creating a profit...for them and for JPI.

That is not an example of just-in-time technological training, but it certainly was just in time to rescue a win-win personnel situation that was going bad for no good reason. The nature of JPI's integrated auto-parts business plan meant that much technology-specific continuing education could be done in-house, the way our German unit worked with staff in Grand

Haven. Community colleges, however, offer excellent ac-
cessibility for manufacturers with plants scattered about the
country, often in small cities and even semi-rural areas. The
junior colleges are not only geographically accessible, relatively affordable, with minimal bureaucracy and strong ties
to…well, they aren't called *community* colleges for nothing.

As competitors for tuition dollars, two-year schools generally are delighted to develop synergy with local employers.
As grassroots educators, most are willing to develop new programs specifically designed for a new business in town, or for
an old business with new technology issues. At JPI, though
we took care of our own group training for new processes or
machinery, we paid employees' tuition for any college-based
training that related to the workplace, be it in engineering
or accounting or management. And we paid *any* vocational
training tuition for laid-off workers during their first year of
a job search.

Community colleges are not America's most glamorous
post-secondary educational institutions. But they are vital,
and they should become more vital. I have been out of touch
with that scene for two decades, but I know four-year institutions have begun to partner with two-year schools to build
networks stressing preparation for the regional workplace—
nursing, for example, where health-care is a major employer.
Small manufacturing operations looking for a new plant location put that kind of educational access on a short list of site
priorities. Response among the more nimble two-year schools
is already happening. We need more of that, with access to
quickly custom-made science and technology curricula. And
we need the paradigm to trickle upward to four-year colleges
and universities in every way more advanced rapid response
education to technological advances can be enhanced. Not an

original idea.   It is happening.   But it needs to be intensified. The public needs to be aware of this synergy, needs to know the stakes involved.   Good things happen when good ideas have broad support.

These are simple examples of an American education system responding to specific job-training needs down at the retail level, where the "just-in-time" concept can work efficiently.   It's a template that also can be viewed from within the philosophy of continuous change—which clearly is a fact as much as it is a way of thinking.   The institutions that fail and crumble sooner rather than later, whether taken in the broadest historical scope or within the much shorter timeline of an era, are the institutions that insist on static goals, insist on static ways of reaching goals, insist on fealty to "grandpa's idea."

Pretend for a moment that the greatest influence on contemporary life, technology, is a static thing.   Technology is the least unchanging thing imaginable, but try to imagine it anyway.   Even lacking new ways of designing things, making things, marketing things and using things, one hopes change in the form of "social progress" would occur.   We saw a great deal of that, for example, between the invention of the wheel and the invention of the steam engine.   I am one who raises both eyebrows at some "legislation" that emanates from our court system.   Yet it is also inarguably true that the only way our great Constitution has worked, and can continue to work, is via a certain amount of flexible interpretation.   Our national touchstone, technology, cannot be static.   Let us not forget that the founders themselves waited a mere two years before massively editing the Constitution with the Bill of Rights…and that the Boston Red Sox won the World Series four times (and even the Chicago Cubs won it twice) before American women were allowed to vote.   The spirit of the founders' Constitution, its grand sweep wrapping federalism and unprecedented individual rights into the same system of government, is indeed indelible. But the founders' own genius for flexibility has prevented the document from falling onto history's trash heap with other lifeless documents.

Channeling continuous change toward positive and productive ends is an excellent definition of progress. Good business managers understand this and stress a parallel dynamic within their workforce, generally known as "continuous improvement." I once adapted the idea into a little book for my own employees entitled *Better Makes Us Best*. Research showed, by the way, that lower-level workers were most likely to have read the book. For sure, any institution that seeks to thrive and grow must steer itself across the seas of change rather than try to build a dike and hide, unaffected by such a powerful force. That includes our largest and greatest institutions of learning, which to my observation are doing quite a decent job of continuous improvement.

In this new era, all educational institutions—from your local high school physics class and community college, to the nation's finest Ph.D programs in our finest graduate schools—must give priority to those new Three R's and pursue them without fail. As professional educators they are uniquely suited to finding ways to meet the challenge. All of us, however, can see the goal: a crucial need for our educational system to reform, refocus, and respond. Global competition, the great driver of the 21st Century business world, will be reaching into and relying upon academia in ways and to depths never before encountered. Just like today's students, all of us will need as much STEM as we can get.

CHAPTER SEVEN

The agony of collateral damage

If America's value-added manufacturing sector thrives, supported by robustly refocused educational and technological research support, then our technology and industry and educational institutions will remain the envy of the world. That would cover three 21st Century benchmark vectors and propel us into the fourth, where—unless we mess things up—we would indeed emerge as a success story in the new global technological world. The foremost reasons to fear failure are the aforementioned matters of a limp national will and government's tendency to serve government by preferring to grow government rather than grow the economy. In this chapter, though, let's assume America executes a successful landing not on the moon but in this new world. And let's talk about the enormous piece of bad news we will encounter—already are encountering—even if our 21st Century becomes a success story. Our society seems not yet willing to discuss the matter. Discuss it we must—now—or our economic victory will be chaotic, bittersweet, and perhaps even pyrrhic.

That bad news, of course, is the prospect of irreversible advances in technology demolishing old concepts of what it means to work for a living, what "full employment" means, and how to sustain a participatory socioeconomic system—how, in other words, to provide opportunity for all Americans to be productive, fulfilled citizens. This is not small stuff, not something that can be addressed with a wave of a political wand from either side of the aisle. This problem needs to be examined and defined in serious public discourse rather than in sparsely populated corners of academia or in shouted and broadcast sound bites. After defining the problem we need to solve it as best we can. This is a revolution, and we should make it as bloodless as possible. Judging by the new normal for political rhetoric ("divisive" seems such an insufficient term), I can only wish us all good luck. I have yet to hear any sound bites that even put this enormous problem on the table.

One *big* footnote before getting on with it: Once everyone understands that this problem looms large and genuine and is not a science-fiction story, then today's gloomy employment picture will be revealed to be what it is. That is a good thing, because it might get that whale-sized red herring removed from public debate.

Like all revolutions, this one did not begin overnight. Anyone who understands technology's forward march must at times have wondered what society will do as less and less human labor is required to meet our needs. I said earlier that younger readers will live in or near this oncoming brave new world. The nature of change is such that even the youngest reader will still be able, in old age, to ask the question technology has always prompted and will forever prompt: "What won't they think of next—and *how will it change my life?*" I think nearly everyone must agree that, over the centuries, most life-changing aspects of technology clearly have been, on balance, positive. The contemporary timeline of the technology revolution, however, has been knocking on many doors in personal ways far more life-changing than the farm-to-factory upheaval that began more than 100 years ago.

One might argue that the farm-to-factory revolution "only"

transferred Americans from rural to urban lifestyles and gave them a pay raise for their troubles. Identities were changed, not atomized. Livelihoods were enhanced. Industrial fallow periods mimicked the farm-based drama of drought and flood. Workdays did not disappear; they merely became fewer and shorter (though less airy). Change was vast, troublesome for many in degrees ranging from minor to traumatic, and it transformed our culture. But, like a self-sealing car tire that runs over a nail, our ship of state and our economy kept right on going and growing. Manufacturing-driven growth meant a need for more workers. It was the American Century. Who could imagine a growing economy that did *not* need more employees? Welcome to the 21st Century, and our current political-social-economic train wreck.

It seems to me that the carnage should be triaged as follows. First, resuscitate the free-market economy and get it growing again—because otherwise all further rescue attempts will be futile. Second, spare no effort to get out the defibrillators and jumpstart that nascent synergy of education reform and tech-based, value-added manufacturing. Those first two choices, subjects of the previous two chapters here, are obvious and—in conception if not execution—easy. Part three of the triage is readily visible for anyone willing to see it, but lacks that kind of clarity. It is a life-threatening socioeconomic condition that is likely to be worsened, rather than ameliorated, by political intervention. The proper course of treatment is no easy call. An operation of some sort will be required, but competing teams of political surgeons are certain to disagree on where to make the incision, and neither team shows any sign of getting it right. Looking at this one from an engineering rather than a political-surgical perspective, let me use this chapter to describe the problem. I'll even have a few words to say about a solution.

For centuries humans have been defined, and have defined themselves, by their craft, their trade, their profession—their *job*. When not sleeping or eating, we spend most of our time on the job. Most of us spend further precious time getting to the workplace. We have distant relatives or friends of friends about whom we know almost nothing except "what they do" (and ancestors we identify by what they *did*). A great-grandfather owned a feed store in Iowa. A quality-control guy where you work has a friend who is a plumber, whose brother the electrician has a daughter in your daughter's grade-school class. Three guys in a tub will never be remembered as Pete, Tom, and John, but will be immortalized as a butcher, a baker and a candlestick maker. "Who lives in that house across the street? Joe Smith. Oh, you mean who *is* he? He works in the prosecutor's office." Our jobs and careers are, to the outside world, the essence of our single-sentence biographies and, one day, the first paragraph of our obituaries.

Self-worth, productivity, the psychology of being a useful citizen…a very powerful battery of attributes is wrapped up in this business of "having a job." I leave it to the psychologists and sociologists to describe these things in clinical and historical detail. But we all have a visceral understanding of both the individual and societal meaning of being defined by *what we do*. We all know—from direct observation or literature or drama or, perish the thought, personal experience—what happens to the psyche of someone who believes he or she is (so much irony to this next word, in context of an essay about technology) *obsolete*. For someone who is, let's say, 60 years old and whose once-revered or at least respected craft suddenly and literally *is* obsolete, the psychological impact has to be devastating for all but a tiny minority who possess superhuman resilience.

A job, then, is a massively important thing to a human being, even without mentioning the more pragmatic essence of what employment is about. If you think the psychology of being employed seems too far afield for this discussion (I obviously don't see it that way), let's have a look at the more practical view of why employment statistics always have been a prime topic conversation and source of smiles or frowns, in venues from your local coffee shop to the White House.

Take a modest annual income (by American standards), and multiply it by the number of years in the workplace. Even a person earning that modest income usually is amazed at the cumulative size of his or her greatest fiscal asset. What comprises a modestly middle-class income these days? Let's say a $50,000 annual income as averaged across a 40-year career. That person on retirement day might well reflect that he earned two million dollars in his lifetime. He might then glance at the compound interest charts, and say, "Let's have a re-do." My point is not to preach thrift (though that is never a bad idea), but to note the kind of individual socioeconomic power many millions of Americans possessed across the 20th Century. Let's see: Three square meals a day, a solid roof overhead, a car in the driveway, a means to raise a family, a few toys, an occasional vacation—not to mention a path to achievement and pride and *identity*. What more could a person ask?

That's the individual view. An imaginary satellite camera image of employment's socioeconomic impact is even more stunning. Henry Ford did not decree the five-dollar day so his workers could buy those Model T's, but it did work out that way. An American economy humming along with an economically meaningful job for everyone who wants one translates into a prosperity picture unlike anything ever seen anywhere else on Earth.

We are not some tiny population made wealthy by oil wells, and not some small, homogeneous, mountaintop nation whose needs can be met by banking and tourism. We are almost four million square miles, the third largest nation by both land mass and population. We are one of the most ethnically diverse nations. Our bloodiest war was fought between our own North and South. But 100 years after that conflict our economic might and national unity allowed us to play a deciding role in the *world's* bloodiest war, freeing much of the globe's population from maniacal fascist regimes.

A quarter century after World War II, zooming that imaginary satellite image in on one of Ike's interstate highways would have revealed auto factory workers headed north towing boats (in summer) or snowmobiles (in winter) bound for second homes in northern Michigan. Two decades later Alan Greenspan was not watching traffic on I-75 when he famously spoke of "irrational exuberance." But that *was* irrational exuberance towing large toys north for those long weekends. That irrational outlier of a "working class" image nonetheless demonstrates the breathtaking power of America's economic engine at full throttle. Still further, that image portrays how such breathtaking power can generate wondrously erroneous calibrations of personal and corporate economic reach. If the image were not so realistic, one could easily see a road sign proclaiming: "You Are Now Leaving the 20th Century." Down on the ground it is an image about unsustainable employment, the thing John McCain was talking about when he said a lot of disappeared car industry jobs "are not coming back."

I said earlier that no politician and no constituency wants to accept this kind of truth. Too bad, because the truth that needs acknowledging is far larger than the American Three automakers shedding jobs, or one entire industry shedding some jobs. It is about structural change, not a cyclical down-turn. We *must* go about the business discussed in the previous two chapters. Those first two steps of the train-wreck triage are a matter of survival. But we must *not* kid ourselves—or let the politicians kid us—into believing that a successful landing in the new global economy will put all those boats and snowmobiles back onto I-75.

So where is the good news in all of this? You heard me profess to have a tendency toward optimism, even in the face of bad news. So what's to be optimistic about?

First, from the perspective of personal experience, as a young boy during the Nazi invasion of Crete I headed for the hills with my caretaker aunt, dodging bullets in the first part of our flight. It was only because of her indomitable spirit, innate intelligence, and ability to forage and bargain that our little household of two middle-aged sisters and two orphaned brothers survived four years of German occupation—plus several years of civil chaos and hardship after the war. Millions of people in the world at that time had it worse. But my wartime childhood suggests that facing America's current problems, armed with America's assets, is a situation that at least *should* leave room for optimism.

Second, in a battlefield crisis there is no substitute for a well-conceived holding action that buys time and guarantees that at the very least you will be around, and prepared, for the decisive action to come. We have a clear path to preparing for full-bore global economic competition; and if this economy does prepare, that means we likely will prevail. As a battlefield metaphor that is most definitely an optimistic scenario. The trouble with battlefield metaphors is that, if honest, they address issues such as "acceptable casualties." In this case I prefer to phrase it as "unavoidable casualties." That is the enormous piece of bad news in the first paragraph of this chapter. The optimist in me says that if we make an honest assessment of the problem and proceed accordingly, we will emerge in the heart of the 21st Century economically victorious—or at least the very best we can be. The pessimist in me says it is very likely that empty political promises will tempt an overreaction to the bad news, leaving government, not the people, as the winner. The better path *is* do-able, so I prefer leaning toward optimism.

What is the first step, assuming that (as we stipulated at the chapter's outset) the first two steps of the triage will be undertaken and accomplished? American leadership—in education, politics, and news media—must convey the onrushing facts of technological progress, including the negative side. Most importantly, the demagoguery must stop. No one should be asked to believe that government, for example, can play entrepreneur and create competitively viable, sustainable new "green jobs" that will clean up the bad numbers on our employment balance sheet. And no one, speaking of demagoguery from the other side, should be asked to believe that a tax cut here and a tax cut there will somehow get the economy humming and put a paycheck in every pocket.

We must accept and deal with the fact that large numbers of Americans will *never* again have jobs providing the kind of income they once earned. We must acknowledge that many Americans now in their 60s or 50s possess once valuable skills that are now obsolete, and that many of these workers will never again, for various reasons, earn a middle-class wage. We must admit that a significant number of Americans who once held "decent jobs" will never again work in any traditional employment setting. We must understand that this trend will only continue—that those workers with science and tech skills will dominate the employment rolls, but that the labor force will require fewer and fewer salaried or hourly workers of *any* background. Can I, or anyone else, quantify these numbers today, and having done so can we draw a curve showing their inexorable march upward on a specific time-line? No. Or rather, no one could do so with any accuracy. No matter. Such numbers aren't needed. The trend and its general destination are evident truths, and we must accept them.

I have yet to hear any sound bites that even put this enor-mous problem on the table. Have you? Surely you have read or heard countless news stories, and watched countless guests on news talk shows, and heard countless politicians shout-ing "Jobs! Jobs! Jobs!" In the course of all that verbosity, have you ever heard anyone say, in paraphrase: "Technologi-cal advancements will mean fewer and fewer workers will be needed. You know what? We are going to have a huge structural problem in what to do with all these 'unneeded' people!" I don't think so. Instead, with the leading edge of this revolution at hand, one is more likely to hear, too many times to count, another debate on whether unemployment benefits should be extended past *two years*. And speaking of structural problems in the workforce, these debates seldom, if ever, mention the fact that *under*employed Americans work-ing multiple part-time jobs are not eligible to receive a single week of unemployment benefits. An underemployed store clerk is every bit as much a part of this big picture as someone whose high-paid factory job has been rendered obsolete. In some cases, of course, the underemployed store clerk *is* a for-merly high-paid worker, factory or otherwise.

Which brings us back, I believe, to employment's founda-tional place in our individual and national psyche, to Ameri-cans' collective anxiety about the future, and to the political possibilities for any skilled demagogue who seeks to bluster his way to election and re-election with promises of "getting this country back on track." Name one politician of either major party who does *not* promise to get this country back on track. The American public will run a gauntlet—this election year and into the foreseeable future—of politicians lined up on either side ignoring truths that make voters uncomfortable, unfriendly, or even angry—truths such as industries maturing, becoming efficient, and shrinking their workforces...or the impossibility of continuing to manufacture obsolete products or products that can never again be made profitably in this country...or the fact that cities and regions that don't diversify, no matter how many "hard-working Americans" live there, cannot avoid a radical, unexpected shift in fortunes.

These kinds of truths routinely get trumped at the ballot box when laid-off voters, or voters afraid of being laid off, or voters with a misconstrued idea of why their friends were laid off, see a political commercial featuring video of a closed factory, an unemployed worker, and an alleged connection—however tenuous or even fictional or even outrageously skewed—to a demagogue's political opponent. That is one tough room in which to be trying to explain the unstoppable and irreversible tide of technological advance, the futility (and wrongheadedness) of trying to sidestep global competition, and—do you want to give this one a try?—*unavoidable casualties*. That is, however, exactly the kind of political honesty we need right now. Have you seen any?

I ask that question no matter what, if any, solutions a politician might go on to offer. One should, after all, define problems before offering solutions. Let's imagine a politician who believes all our problems could be solved by nationalizing every American business, right down to your local dry cleaner and 7-Eleven, and by handing some kind of federal transfer payment to every U.S. citizen. In other words, let's imagine a delusional candidate for office whose 100 pounds of problem-solving do not contain half an ounce of valid ideas. I would *still* give this guy credit for prefacing his delusions with a clear and accurate statement that new technology and a new global economic paradigm—*not* an evil entrepreneurial class—have been laying the groundwork for a shrinking, restructured workforce. Most everything this candidate had to say would strike me as silly in concept and utter disaster if executed. And I would say, "Well, he's crazy, but at least he knows what problem he thinks he is trying to solve." This mythical politician is less delusional than much of the political rhetoric and media commentary we hear these days, which does not acknowledge the core problem.

Everyone who cares about these matters has seen numbers from unimpeachable sources—in academia and in government bureaucracy and in think tanks—stating the percentage of federal income tax paid by affluent Americans. One can wiggle such numbers a fraction of a percent in one direction or another, depending on the definitions and parameters one chooses to use. But it is undeniably true that many Americans (at least 40 percent) pay no federal income tax at all, and that top earners pay a *lot* of federal income tax (one estimate says the top 10 percent of earners pay more than 70 percent of federal income tax revenue). It is also undeniably true that further soaking the rich would not solve this country's fiscal problems even if the Treasury sent armored cars around to empty bank accounts belonging to the top one percent. And *still*, various sellers are finding buyers for T-shirts that proclaim: WE ARE THE 99 PERCENT. God bless the marketplace.

A lot of money has been fairly earned in the last few decades. Meanwhile, a widening income disparity has emerged among Americans. The misguided and misinformed have set those two facts down side by side, added one plus one, and come up with the demagogic numbers *du jour*—one percent and ninety-nine percent. Other facts we have been discussing here appear meaningless to those who seem stridently intent, blinders in place, to substitute class warfare for public discourse. It is as if entry-level detectives had come into a room, spotted two clues, and closed their case Clouseau-like without looking at a large-caliber smoking gun on the table. You know my experience and views regarding free markets, entrepreneurialism, the need to create new wealth, and the inability of governments to handle the job. I'm game for a spirited response to those 99 PERCENT T-shirts, and you'll find it in Chapter Nine. Here I want to stay close to the script, because someone needs to call full attention to that smoking gun, and to the fact that it will be an even larger weapon—much larger—before this drama ends.

Technological progress, I repeat, is neither a hero nor a villain. It is what it is—which is merely the most powerful force on earth short of nuclear warfare (which is, of course, old technology) or implosion of our sun (which, depending on your view, drives either nature's technology or a creator's technology). Rapid-paced technological advances are the reason a 21st Century economy can grow without producing enough new jobs to allow a consumer economy to recover from any recession, let alone from the longest recession anyone can recall. How incredibly unfortunate we are entering an era of unprecedented technological progress even as housing values undergo massive restructuring, even as what happens in Spain or Greece matters to the U.S., even as what happens in China matters *a lot* to the

U.S., even as we—and everyone else—are embarking on a new adventure in globalized economic interrelationships (all made possible by new technology).

We don't know what the "jobs picture" will look like on the other side of the first two triage steps this chapter assumes will be taken and will be successful. All we know is that if those steps are not taken, no new jobs will be created and millions more of the old jobs will disappear. That will leave not much of our economic house remaining except some damaged supporting walls, which will begin falling in on each other. This, to offer the largest understatement found in these pages, is not a situation in which class warfare will be helpful. What will be helpful is to study new technology's impact on the workplace, and to hypothesize what to do about it. My own thoughts always come back to the idea that the word "jobs" is becoming as obsolete as many 20th Century jobs themselves. Which, as I have suggested, makes "Jobs! Jobs! Jobs!" an eerie sort of rant.

In recent years we have heard much talk about more and more Americans becoming entrepreneurs. Clearly that has happened, but it defies quantification. The small businesses that are touted as job creators are not what most people regard as "small" businesses. A company with hundreds of workers is classified as a "small" business. If a company with, say, 100 employees is one of those Vector Two tech-driven companies on its way up, then it can be a serious job creator. The number of entrepreneurs who own companies with a workforce of, say, 100 or more is relatively small. On the other hand, how many Americans do you suppose have gone into business lately on their own—literally *on their own*? I doubt anyone can honestly estimate the number of people who are doing landscaping, or computer consulting, or specialized regional sales representation, or any number of both manual and technical occupations either all alone or with minimal hired help. I suspect you would agree it is a very high number. I suspect it is a growing number, and I suspect a higher percentage are finding success than in decades past—technology, especially communications technology, being the prime reason.

Amid the economic landscape of deep recession, this sort of creative self-employment runs parallel to one of the few good things that have been happening lately in Greece. My native land has long been one of the most bureaucratized, inefficient, over-governed economies in the world. Greece once had a state-owned flagship international carrier, Olympic Airlines, serving routes in more than 30 countries. The government asked me to consult with the ministry that operated Olympic and to offer advice on solving its deep fiscal problems. The problems, as it turned out, didn't require much analysis. Olympic could have continued successful operation but for one difficulty: It employed at least two and perhaps three times as many employees as necessary to fly well and provide excellent service. Furthermore, many of the extra employees performed no Olympic-related chores except to cash their paychecks. None. My advice was obvious, but politically unacceptable, so it was ignored. Olympic eventually went out of business, then re-emerged as a small, privatized regional carrier.

With that kind of economic culture it is no accident that Greece wound up, at this writing, as a deeply indebted nation near total collapse, where people live in deep fear of the future (and, it should be noted, more than a few people far away from Greece fear the repercussions of a bad ending in Athens). The one piece of good news I hear lately is a surge in entrepreneurial activity, ranging from laid-off workers turned shopkeepers in the cities to provincial farmers who, instead of marketing their potatoes to a middleman, are bringing them directly to market—where consumers are paying less money for fresher potatoes. It would take far too much space to explain the history or to attempt a current-events report of what is happening in Greece. I share my old countrymen's concern. But the self-generated "jobs" movement has been, so far, an encouraging thing.

I do *not* foresee America solving its problems by farmers bringing potatoes into the cities while every laid-off autoworker opens a coffee shop. But neither do I foresee that spirit *not* playing a major role here as technology continues to "lay off" workers on into the next generation. My important point here is that we—Americans and their government—need to see what is happening rather than invent politically useful narratives that don't just misstate but totally ignore technology's growing and irreversible impact. For the president and his administration to talk a great deal about the role of community colleges is, for example, a fine thing. But to suggest, even tacitly, that a burst of educational reform will lead to anything resembling full employment is pure silliness. It takes fewer people these days to build a car or to bake an economic pie. We do need tech-savvy workers to get it done, and we do need that educational reform, but it's a separate proposition from making the workforce grow as *much* as we'd like. Closely related, but separate. Let's get the educational system on track, let's keep our technological supremacy in place, let's do all we can to assure capital is available for value-added manufacturing in sectors where we can compete. But let's do so without pretending our very large army of laid-off workers will all come marching back to the payroll, and that all of those who do will enjoy the same lifestyle. It simply cannot happen, and we cannot let a futile effort to make it happen drag the entire economy down toward collapse.

My thought is that we can restructure the economy and get it growing at a useful pace again, with workforce levels future historians will regard as remarkably good considering the timeline in technological history. And while all this is happening, we need to prepare for long-term technological progress by reinventing the meaning of the word "job." We need to save our constantly evolving capitalist economic engine, which means sustaining it as a free-market organism rather than a new department of the federal government. That's one side of a ledger I deeply believe to be the real bottom line. The other side of the ledger requires recognizing that today's new income disparities are genuine, and that if we wish to maintain our free-market economic engine, then we must make repairs so *it*, and not the government, brings a level of prosperity to everyone willing to pursue it. Why? Because government can*not* get that job done. No large, diverse nation's government ever has done so successfully, and this government is uniquely designed to achieve prosperity the American way.

Either we make capitalism work for the 21st Century, or we—all of us—lose. How badly do we lose? In my view, the decisions our society makes in that regard will be the most important the republic has made since the Constitution was written. No matter what kind of restructuring our society faces, we must continue to *create* wealth. If we do not keep creating new wealth, the income discrepancies we now see will be a sociologist's picnic by comparison. The economic pie, whatever its size, is created by those at the top—and, more accurately and specifically, by the system that allows those with capital to create more capital. That system is not working as well as it used to. Fix it. Now. Get prepared for the 21st Century before everyone, from Warren Buffett to a steelworker who has not had a job for three years, wonders where the last piece of pie has gone. Get that pie growing again.

Don't get the government any more deeply involved in passing the pie around than Washington already is. Retool capitalism and invent new ways for anyone who wishes to contribute to do so creatively, creating a place for himself or herself at the table. Give some real thought—as in structured discourse as spirited as the founders in Philadelphia more than 200 years ago—to what is meant by "everyone becoming an entrepreneur." Somewhere in and around that idea just might lie the viable approach to making "We, the people" and "a more perfect union" resonate in a globally connected world.

If you still lean in the direction of soaking the rich, I have a plan for doing it the right way. I think it's fair, and I think you might agree. I believe it will produce positive results for all, and will help with all aspects of that economic pie. That's Chapter Ten.

First, a few words in defense of globalization.

CHAPTER EIGHT

It's a connected globe.
We're all on it.
It's that simple.

America's large and vocal army of economic isolationists has dwindled to battalion strength, at least among those who take the 21ˢᵗ Century seriously. The holdouts are contemporary Don Quixote's. What windmills might they tilt at? Cargo containers, perhaps. Or integrated circuits. A few could camp in the deepest woods and become hunter-gatherers, crafting their arrows and footwear. Only that kind of isolationism *might* allow someone to opt off the new global grid. Anyone who remembers the '60s counterculture and *The Whole Earth Catalogue,* with its epiphanous cover photo of our planet viewed from space, will appreciate the irony. New technology—not communal living or rock and roll or "progressive" politics—is bringing all 7 billion of us together. Unavoidably, irreversibly. We are becoming brothers in commerce, at least. Progress on other fronts will continue to require a great deal of work.

This is not to say an overwhelming majority of Americans understand or even accept the new reality. As with numerous vital issues of our times, "globalization" became a buzzword, stoked some anger, then went quiet in a corner. Not silent, just quiet, off political radar. In our lifetimes, the loudest and most memorable buzz for economic nationalism came from the

1992 presidential campaign of independent candidate H. Ross Perot. The North American Free Trade Agreement, Perot said in a televised debate with then-President George H.W. Bush and rival Bill Clinton, would create a "giant sucking sound" of American jobs and industry fleeing to Mexico. Perot told the same audience that loss of industry and jobs to foreign countries was "Number One on my agenda," a sentiment that won him 19 percent of all votes cast, the best outcome by a third-party candidate since Teddy Roosevelt in 1912. The quirky Perot received almost 20 million votes despite announcing his candidacy on the Larry King TV talk show, dropping out of the race in July, and then re-entering just a month before the election.

Although Perot's campaign theme song was Willie Nelson's "Crazy," there was nothing crazy about his ability to recognize the electorate's fear of American industry disappearing offshore. Twenty years later, despite dialing the volume down, we have not progressed a great deal toward understanding and coping with 21st Century economics. It almost seems the public mood knows only two frequencies: ranting Perot-like against irreversible economic forces, or stoically waiting for whatever happens next. Passive response to THE TECHNOLOGY IMPERATIVE is *not*, I am sure you have noticed, the reason I emphasize the unavoidable and irreversible nature of high-tech progress. To the contrary, my point is we must become proactive in our response—we need to become, top to bottom, the most techno-friendly and techno-savvy nation we possibly can be. That especially includes the manufacturing sector Perot and his followers worried about the most. I, too, have had serious concerns about preserving and growing U.S. manufacturing activity—*technology-driven, value-added* manufacturing.

It's worth a quick look, by the way, across the very border

that was the focal point of the NAFTA debate. A thumbnail survey regarding the U.S., Mexico, and the industry whose every sneeze infects the American economy with a cold, reveals a giant sucking sound, for sure. The sound is coming, however, from all directions.

As of this writing, Mexico's longstanding automotive best-seller is in fact manufactured in Mexico, where Nissan has been building a virtually unchanged model since the very year of Perot's presidential shooting star. One of the few changes in the Tsuru (you know it as an old-generation Sentra) is a new transmission by Renault. The Mexican-built Tsuru and its French-built transmissions are exported to the Middle East and Africa in a cheaper model that lacks, among other things, a catalytic converter, which Mexico, like the U.S., requires. Mexico's No. 2 seller is a Volkswagen also assembled in Mexico (as was the last VW Beetle ever made). The No. 3 seller is another Mexican-built Nissan product. No. 4 is the first American nameplate on the list, the compact Chevrolet Aveo, made in Mexico—but let's not forget the Aveo was originally made by a General Motors partner in South Korea. The Chevrolet Spark, a popular seller south of the border, is *still* made in South Korea. Ford's F150 pickups sold in Mexico are all made south of the border, but Ford Explorers for the Mexican market are manufactured in Illinois. Dodge makes a popular product in Detroit for the Mexican market under the same name, ironically, that it is sold in America—the Durango. Volkswagen and Toyota sell popular models in Mexico that are made in Brazil.

Meanwhile, vehicles manufactured in Mexico and shipped north are a statistical blip. Soccer moms might be aware, though, that every Chrysler/Dodge minivan sold in the United States is now built in Canada—a nation that,

like the U.S., has modern pollution regulations and its own
United Auto Workers union...but also has, some would note,
lower health-care costs.

Some near-impossible calculus is involved here. A typical
car contains more than 30,000 parts. Some of these are literally "nickel and dime," such as interior fabric fasteners. Some
are the very newest technology, such as onboard computers.
Some *use* the very newest technology to make, for example,
composite materials. Typically *none* of these parts is made at
the site where the car is assembled. One "American" vehicle
might contain parts manufactured in 20 U.S. states and several foreign countries—just as vehicles assembled in Canada
might contain more American parts than Canadian parts. Is
there a better illustration of the futility in any attempt to sidestep the connectivity of today's global commerce? Or why
a company that engineers, designs, assembles, and markets
a 30,000-part product, much of it time-sensitive high-tech,
would tend to keep its technology stream close by its manufacturing operations?

Money, unless confiscated, pays no heed to borders. Capital flows to any opportunity. Competitive factors sort genuine
opportunity from mere wishful thinking and help estimate a
risk/reward ratio. Free markets lubricate that paradigm and
keep it running efficiently. Seeking to quarantine dollars at
home in America and to keep competitive goods out of this
country is, in the context of free markets, asinine. We have
international trade referees to monitor cases of, for example,
a government-controlled economy "dumping" goods here at a
loss just to keep dollars flowing out and to keep its own workers employed. We know from historical experience what happens when protectionist policies are allowed to corrupt market
forces, sometimes even launching trade wars. That historical

experience, awful as it was, occurred long before a product ordered today from Singapore could be in Los Angeles—or destinations in 100 other countries—tomorrow. And long before a supply disruption of one part among 30,000 could stop an automotive assembly line, make an industry sneeze, and give the world's largest economy a cold. One does not smooth out globalized business disagreements by taking one's ball and bat and going home.

It is no stretch to say that "globalization" began occurring as soon as man found a way to move goods, and himself, beyond the nearest village. The communities founded by ancient Greeks in Sicily and near what is now Marseilles, for example, were examples of human resources being invested in commercial opportunities—making a living, in other words. Coastal cultures all around the Mediterranean traded across what was, to them, the known world. Well before the birth of Christ, Phoenicians crisscrossed the Mediterranean in galleys, trading in the dye used to create the purple of royalty and spreading their invention, the alphabet. Galleys and dye both represented—though it's a difficult concept to understand in these high-tech days—new technology. Commerce being commerce, it found a way to apply these technologies in free markets. Bingo—world trade! A much smaller world, but world trade nonetheless.

Communities the Greeks established on islands and on much of the Mediterranean coast could rightly be called colonies because the founders traveled—by standards of the day—a long way to set up shop. But the Greeks, never much for concentrating power effectively, did not emphasize what today is fashionably (and accurately) called "extractive" colonies. The Greeks were not, like the Spanish conquistadores, on a mission to loot a continent, seize resources by any means,

and return home with the goods. The broad swath of coloni-
zation, from the Romans to the British (who really *did* establish a presence across the entire globe), unfolded in a range
of behaviors from savage to benign to arguably beneficial,
always with great cultural impact. Even the Spaniards left
their language as a legacy in all but four nations of North and
South America. In retrospect this was globalization the hard
way, but it was globalization.

From the discovery of fire to the invention of whatever is
being invented this very afternoon, time gaps between major
discoveries have become shorter and shorter. Communication
has become instantaneous. Physical transport has shortened
on trans-Atlantic routes from being impossible, to more than
a month (Columbus), to less than eight hours from Detroit
to Paris. A 1st Century Roman or even a late 19th Century
American would be, if set down at JFK Airport or even at a
McDonald's window table in any Midwest small town, ines-
timably bewildered. Across such a tableau of rapid and accelerating change it seems *everything* has become obsolete
or at least obsolescent—technology, products, "solid" information, political boundaries, and physics textbooks (some of
which were used by students still alive today) explaining why
it will be impossible for man ever to reach the moon. Every
advancement through the centuries impacted culture, directly
or indirectly. Even "impossible" ventures (sailing across the
Atlantic, or to the moon) were revealed to be inevitable once
capital was expended to that end. Finding ways to transmit
audiovisual signals from the surface of the moon has much
more than a little to do with 21st Century "globalization."

Perhaps only one thing has not become at least a little bit
obsolete from the Phoenicians until now and on into future
known worlds. That is, the wealth- and prosperity-creating

power of free markets. New business ideas will find a way for new technology to fill a niche, no matter how far away or how protected someone may believe the niche to be. Solutions to problems in commerce and industry will, as always, be the holy grail of the entrepreneur—who will call those problems "opportunities." If that old cliché ever had a transformational application, this new era is it. My main purpose here, in fact, is to warn against a very strong possibility that America's prosperity and preeminence will fall victim not to "globalization" but to inertia, to bad definitions of "problem" and "opportunity," and to zero-sum politics promising voters that emasculating an economy will somehow yield rewards. The national decisions we make right now will determine far more than the mere difference between a profitable venture and a business gone sour. Choosing in the wrong direction will lead to the direst consequences for an entire nation. Choosing in the right direction will lead at least to the best deal possible, and could turn out to be the best thing that has happened to America since the founders' handiwork.

The world is not being colonized all over again, but the globe is being discovered—and discovering itself—in brand-new ways. This time no swords are being drawn, no cannon fired. This new wave of excursions across the planet is not about gaining sovereignty over other peoples' real estate and treasure. In the main, these are not even government-sponsored expeditions. They are all about the movement of private capital throughout open societies around the world, about who will do this most successfully in terms of prosperity for their own economy and their own people back home, and about whether America will retain technological pre-eminence within a free-market capitalist system—and thereby sustain its global economic reach.

It is even about access to information, then development of business ideas, and then the movement and application of capital in countries that have *not* been open societies. Many of us remember when Richard Nixon's trip to China was seen as a momentous first step across the "Bamboo Curtain." We had no idea that just a few decades later pixels would be carrying billions of messages daily throughout China's "impenetrable" geography, and that attempts to block communications freedom could never again be entirely successful. We certainly didn't expect, when Nixon and Henry Kissinger left for home, that we would live to see General Motors establish hundreds of car dealerships in China, or Buick ranking as China's favorite nameplate, or a product made by Chinese workers being the absolute must-have piece of advanced consumer technology in the United States. How *could* we have seen this? At this writing anyone at least 40 years old was alive at the time of the Nixon visit. However, to illustrate how rapidly contemporary technology and culture advance, in 1972 mass market computers had not yet been developed, the first handheld mobile phone was a year away (let alone being manufactured in Shenzen, as is the iPhone), and "The Godfather" (and its "offer he can't refuse") had just hit the movie screens.

Clearly there is a world of discovery happening right now even though the evening news cannot show us pictures of three little ships landing in the Bahamas, crewed by sailors who think they are in the general neighborhood where Richard Nixon and Mao Zedong would exchange toasts almost 500 years later. Columbus and his sponsors had intercontinental commerce on their minds as surely as we have trade on our minds whenever we contemplate the meaning of globalization. Nixon and Kissinger did not have visions of Buicks driving past the Forbidden City, but these astounding leaps forward have a way of being, in the end, about commerce.

Let me suggest that our ubiquitous old friend the pie chart is as good a way as any to describe what can happen next, which is what should happen next, and certainly is what we *want* to happen next. That is, throughout the 21st Century the United States will *not* have surrendered its title as the world's leading manufacturing nation. Our graduate schools will *still* be attracting science and engineering students from every corner of earth. Our research output will *still* be on the cutting edge for the entire planet. We will have *grown* our currently stagnant economic pie. And in all probability, the *global* economic pie will have grown immensely. In fact, it is difficult to imagine the American pie growing unless the world's pie also grows. It might sound counter-intuitive to many politicians and ideologues, but we are *all* now techno/economic colonists on this interconnected globe. That is why globalization could go in the books as the best thing that happened to America since the founders gave our nation life. If we win in the global arena, we win at home.

I don't wish that assertion to sound either naïve or simplistic. I do want it to sound like an obvious truth, which I believe it to be. But our public and private strategy for America's place in a global economy needs to be well thought-out and strategically implemented. We can't make investments everywhere in the world without evaluating the risks. Capitalism, however, is all about taking intelligent, well-reasoned risks, with profit accruing to—or loss befalling—the risk-takers. Unlike the conquistadores, in the new techno-economic environment we can cross oceans and *create* new wealth rather than merely stealing resources and loading them on the next cargo ship. Commerce and industry have always found mutually beneficial ways of partnering up with another company next door. Now, with ever fewer barriers and with technology allowing ready linkage, there is no reason to avoid partnering on the other side of the planet, and every reason to lead the way in doing so. Why? To keep making America's economic pie larger and larger. If we keep America's competitive leverage intact in the lab and on the shop floor, we will do OK. If we stop growing the economy (which is perilously close to being a fact at this moment), then the United States might never recover.

America has had a consumer economy for a very long time. We entered the new century with consumer spending accounting for 70 percent of GDP. All the more reason that in no way can the chicken-or-the-egg game be played to "blame globalization" for loss of jobs. Not when technology—American technology for the most part—allows assembly lines to use far less labor while producing far more complicated products than our grandparents, and even our parents, consumed. We need to get into full globalization mode as quickly and efficiently and competitively as possible. We need to do so without blaming technology for unavoidable job losses. We need to take an intelligent, informed look at how many lost jobs can be replaced, and what that picture will look like on into the next generation. We need to remind ourselves how new wealth is created to grow our prosperity, and we need to make sure we stop corroding the economic engine that does the heavy lifting. That much is clear.

Time now to talk a bit about why and how that same engine, wondrous as it is, needs retooling if we are to avoid becoming, after our relative 15 minutes of fame on a very lengthy world history timeline, a failed nation.

CHAPTER NINE

First, do no harm

The international terrorist threat has consumed our national will and much of our treasure for more than a decade. Nearly 3,000 people were murdered at the World Trade Center. Almost twice that many American military personnel have been killed in Iraq and Afghanistan. Estimated dollar cost for those two wars approaches $4 trillion. Homeland security concerns have redefined our concept of civil liberties. Terrorism has transformed American life and remains a profound danger that has no foreseeable end. But our discussion here involves a challenge I believe will, if not effectively confronted, pose an even broader national threat. No terrorist, unless he possesses an arsenal of targeted thermonuclear bombs, can reduce America's identity and aspirations to rubble in every ZIP Code. We can do that to ourselves if we continue backing into the new technological era and then, paralyzed by the economic effects of our negligence, surrender our individual and collective destinies to government for safekeeping.

Some readers—*many*, I hope, because I wish these words to reach readers who are not predisposed to my views—will say I have been too simplistic. They will say I am now heaping hyperbole upon oversimplification by calling these matters more dangerous than the terrorist threat. They will say I am constantly apologizing for capitalism's failings. Let me respond directly to these three fairly raised criticisms, because

I want context to be straightforward and clear as we arrive at the heart of my message.

First, I prefer "basic" to simplistic. This little book intentionally contains not a single chart or footnote. You can read it cover to cover (or pixel to pixel) on an average airplane flight. It is, I hope, *easily* read and retained. I want you to keep my basic and sometimes obvious points in mind as you audit the 24/7 information buzz and the endless red-blue, left-right tug of political war. You will see the same gaping hole I see. The lack of urgent discussion regarding technology's impact on our economic and political fabric is astonishing. The core issue—the new technological era's long-term implications for creating and sharing wealth—is not even *mentioned* in mainstream political discourse. A huge amount of thought and resources must be assembled and managed, right now, to address this crisis. That is the reason for this book, and that is why I have made it basic, with no hesitation to note the obvious. One need not describe ocean-floor tectonic science when one's goal is to get people to look up and see a tsunami bearing down. I don't pretend to have detailed solutions. *That* would truly be simplistic. I do wish to offer one concept I believe has promise (Chapter Ten), and which I hope will become the subject of serious discussion.

Second, I don't seek to draw any straight-line mathematical comparisons between these challenges and the danger of terrorism—or the population explosion or global warming or growing viral immunity to antibiotics or anything known or unknown threat. I *am* stating that ignoring the issues raised here will beyond question destroy our economy, dwarfing the 2008 recession's impact upon most Americans. That's without mentioning my concerns about an escalating populist stampede toward disastrous state-centric solutions that will worsen the economic chaos. And that further does not include what I view as potentially the greatest social upheaval since the Civil War, in forms which—like technological advancements—we cannot foretell with any great specificity. So no, I do not think it is hyperbole—when inaction will *guarantee* at minimum economic collapse—to say we are discussing an even greater threat than the considerable threat of terrorism.

Third, American capitalism requires no apology. The recently completed American Century showed the world how free markets provide opportunity to entrepreneurs, whose activities grow the economy and provide opportunity for all others to prosper within that economy. Even during the best of times many have demanded apologies for inequality in the world's foremost *destination* economy—to which the world's downtrodden seek to migrate and thrive. We remain the destination of choice even as our economy performs the least well it has in 80 years. That is why, historically and structurally, I find the idea of apologizing for capitalism to be, let's say, exceedingly counter-intuitive. Meanwhile, yes, our economic engine *has* gone near idle. It has been running worse yet in terms of creating jobs—most citizens' path to prospering while sharing in our uniquely fruitful economy's growth. This new downward economic track is not good. It is not sustainable. It is precisely what this book is about. But this is not a time for apology. It is time to remind what has generated every American generation's prosperity, time for an exhortation to right that good ship rather than scuttle it. Define the problem correctly and we'll be OK. The problem is not capitalism, not free markets, or whatever modified term you might use to designate a thriving economy that is not choked by government interference.

All the issues we have been discussing can be defined

as one basic, solvable problem—plus an overwhelming new problem that will arise if we let a bad definition produce a horribly wrong solution to the first problem. Further, this potential second problem—a foreseeable consequence of a bad choice—would *not* be solvable any more than all the king's horses and all the king's men could put Humpty-Dumpty together again. That is why all our society's engineers—the usual kind plus the economists plus the politicians plus the MBAs plus the butcher, the baker, and the candlestick maker...all of us—must get that first definition right. We must drill down to the underlying problem rather than stopping halfway and firing shotgun blasts at political targets of opportunity. We must, as an athlete or stage performer might say, nail it. No solution can be found by saying, "It's capitalism's fault," then turning things over to government for a while to see how that goes. Nor can we solve anything by saying, "Hey, it's just cyclical; leave it alone and it will take care of itself." Those are two bad solutions in response to bad definitions, the first one proactively catastrophic and the second merely awful in its self-defensive refusal to deal with facts. The first definition ("Capitalism is the problem") will lead us to government-assisted suicide. The other definition ("Hey, it's just cyclical") will guarantee that sooner or later, and probably sooner, society will tire of a slow death, will circle back to the first definition, and will drink the big-government hemlock.

Let me offer a different way to define the problem. It's the title of this book, and—speaking of efficiencies—it characterizes both the problem *and* the solution. If these pages resulted in not much except to introduce THE TECHNOLOGY IMPERATIVE as a common term in public discussion of unemployment, I would be happy enough. It may not thump the political stump as loudly as "Jobs! Jobs! Jobs!" But "THE TECHNOLOGY IMPERA-

TIVE" points toward an actual cause of employment stagnation (rather than "those guys in the other political party"), and toward an actual solution (rather than "getting this country back on track"). It says technology has no ideological or political orientation. It says neither a Democratic nor a Republican platform can alter the fact that Everyman Tool and Die will need 30 percent fewer workers next year to produce the same inventory. It says that even if you nationalize the tool and die industry and try to stop foreign product at the border, employment at Everyman will drop by 30 percent—or more. It says technology has created an ever more global economy. It says that if we want to create jobs that pay a living wage, we need to produce value-added manufacturing goods efficiently and at a globally competitive price. It says we cannot accomplish these things unless our schools find new ways to energize STEM education, and to stream new technology and training to industry on a just-in-time basis. That is THE TECHNOLOGY IMPERATIVE.

So yes, this is all very basic, fundamental, and even obvious to anyone who has been paying attention to a tsunami that can be seen merely by looking upward and outward. But ask yourself, how does this fit what you see and hear in broadcast news and commentary, or in 99.9 percent of widely circulated political verbiage? Answer: not at all. You don't hear it. THE TECHNOLOGY IMPERATIVE is not acknowledged except when camouflaged and submerged deep within the political blame game. It's as if an actual ocean tsunami were best described by its political affiliation. One can easily envision blue and red network commentators standing on a coastal balcony tossing spitballs while ignoring a wall of water we see bearing down on them. That "audience as insider" device has worked well onstage since ancient times, and in cartoons almost since ink was invented. It works here, too, but as a cartoon that makes you want to cry, not laugh.

To get the 21st Century's foremost socioeconomic problem properly defined and onto the workbench for solving we need to separate functional parameters from political prism. Let's expand the stated characteristics of technology. Let's stipulate that not only is technology neither good nor bad, it is neither Democrat nor Republican, neither socialist nor capitalist (though you will see a *lot* more new technology being developed with the aid of free markets). Important new technology arrives on the scene with or without any political party's invitation, and becomes a mighty instrument of change—far mightier than any party or politician. As new technology continues to make business and industry more efficient—not just in the manufacturing sector, but in virtually every service industry and profession imaginable—charlatans, demagogues, and simple ignorant obfuscators discover what might be the all-time perfect "wedge issue." This book is not concerned with the politics; but it does care, very much, about the consequences of misdirected "problem-solving."

Generating new wealth without maintaining current employment levels, let alone increasing employment opportunities, presents dangerous consequences. That describes our current economy—dangerous. It is a problem that must be addressed. Economic growth has been slow or relatively static. Employment numbers are worse and will continue trending downward for *structural* reasons. This already has meant an increasing polarization between economic strata. No one—not even a capitalist, certainly not Henry Ford with his Model T assembly workers—fails to understand that employment accelerates a consumer economy. Workers buy things. Creating private sector jobs is an integral part of distributing wealth broadly even as new wealth is created. Capitalists *love* to create jobs because it distributes wealth without removing the incentives and rewards for risking capital. Entrepreneurs and companies that risk wealth will (if successful) create new wealth, which means creating new jobs, which…it's a never-ending win-win-win proposition. I like to think nearly every American has understood this for a long time, even if not all Americans are willing to concede its functional truth.

But along comes 21st Century technology, with a new global economy in tow. THE TECHNOLOGY IMPERATIVE (the *problem* side of it) will—without any assistance from government *or* entrepreneurs—drain wealth from ordinary citizens and skew relative affluence in ways deeply counter to 20th Century experience and 21st Century aspirations. Free-market capitalism, in the face of new technological efficiencies and marketplace competition, begins to flag in its built-in share-the-wealth mechanism more generally known as employment opportunities. The public sector, meanwhile, long ago has gobbled up a large enough chunk of the economy to create sluggishness. Further meanwhile, health care was largely a government sector and our fastest-growing industry even before Obamacare. Putting a larger percentage of the populace on a government payroll or in receipt of some other transfer payment while fewer and fewer workers foot the entitlement bill for retirees will not work. We would be marching toward insolvency and economic stagnation even if technology could somehow be stuffed back into a genie's bottle rather than arriving as it does, fresh every day, welcomed or not, to further impact the workforce.

This worse-than-stagnant situation cannot be allowed to stand, nor can we let politics mess up the quest for a solution. We must confront THE TECHNOLOGY IMPERATIVE as a separate, non-political issue. We cannot ignore the shrinking economic realities of most working Americans, nor can we pay serious attention to wild rhetoric blaming "the one percent" for lay-offs at Everyman Tool and Die. Somewhere toward the center, as usual, lies the most direct route toward social benefit without disastrous unintended consequences. The only politics I invoke here *is* my only politics, my abiding belief that free markets must be allowed to function as the source of our personal and national prosperity. We must get that capitalist win-win-win cycle of wealth creation and wealth distribution running smoothly again. It is the one institution that can mint both sides of a coin once commonly known as the American Dream—a "living wage" for ordinary workers, and a risk/reward payoff for entrepreneurs who make it happen. Problem-solvers must keep in mind the prime rule imposed upon eager physicians standing by with scalpels in hand: "First, do no harm." In other words in this context: "You can't create golden eggs by killing the goose that lays them."

Previous chapters shared some thoughts about the four benchmark vectors that will measure success regardless of our actions or inaction. I also suggested that if some mechanism—a formally organized and sanctioned policymaking convention, or confederation of public-academic-governmental panels—were tasked to address THE TECHNOLOGY IMPERATIVE, it would be the most important such effort since the founders gathered in Philadelphia. Given the stakes, I do not consider that assertion to be any more hyperbolic than mentioning this crisis in the same breath as international terrorism. Failure to harness THE TECHNOLOGY IMPERATIVE will make nearly all other civic enterprises irrelevant. A carefully chosen and tasked high-profile commission, with a number of issue-specific sub-panels, strikes me as an excellent idea. On the other hand,

I also thought the Simpson-Bowles commission was a good idea for getting the U.S. off square one in solving our sovereign debt crisis. I still think so, as a matter of fact. In any case, creating some kind of mega-horsepower panel to tackle THE TECHNOLOGY IMPERATIVE will, like Simpson-Bowles, be for naught unless national leadership gets out front and *leads*. As noted, the fewer partisan politicians on the panel itself, the better. We all need to help make such a panel or convention or any moral and effective equivalent succeed.

Let's pretend not only that some such a body has been appointed and tasked under whatever authority, but that I have been given a concerned citizen's opportunity to address the gathered assembly. Let's pretend a far more eloquent speaker has preceded me and delivered a brilliant, compelling explanation of what THE TECHNOLOGY IMPERATIVE means. Let's pretend, in fact, that this speaker revealed himself or herself to be the combined equivalent of JFK in his inaugural address, Martin Luther King Jr. in his "I Have a Dream" speech, William Faulkner in his Nobel Prize acceptance speech, Rep. Barbara Jordan in her 1976 Democratic Convention keynote speech, and Ronald Reagan extolling Mr. Gorbachev to "tear down that wall!" He or she would need to be that kind of speaker, because we are going to pretend every person in America, as a result of that oratory, now realizes technology has had and will continue to have dramatic impact on the size and skills of our workforce. Let's further pretend *everyone* realizes technological progress will have this impact whether we elect candidates from the left, the right, men, women, tall people, or short people. That would be one wonderful and important speech, a masterful achievement in the art and science of defining a problem.

So I offer my thanks to that imaginary speaker, and step

forward for my own imaginary presentation regarding THE TECHNOLOGY IMPERATIVE in the long term—which we all know will arrive, because of technology, sooner rather than later. My few extemporaneous minutes of allotted time might be transcribed something like this.

Ladies and gentlemen, it is heartening to see you have gone straight to the real problem, which has everything to do with new technology and nothing to do with ideology and political posturing. If you stay on that straight and narrow path, your outcome will be a good one.

Let me emphasize, though, something you might view as overreach, something you might be tempted to kick down the road for later action. Don't do that. We must start thinking *now* about how to rejuvenate our great old capitalist paradigm for creating and sharing wealth. We all know the system is creaking a bit. I want you to fully understand and ponder the fact that technology ultimately will render the capitalist paradigm, *in its current form,* not merely creaky but unsustainable.

This panel has unanimously affirmed that private-sector risk-taking is where wealth is created, and always will be where wealth is created. Politicians and bureaucrats always say this at ribbon-cuttings, but I have witnessed way too many instances of government acting as if wealth creation deserves punishment rather than encouragement. So if it's no great trouble, would you please re-stipulate for the record, on camera, with no winking and nudging from big-government advocates, the source of all new wealth—and therefore the source of our prosperity? Very good. Thank you.

The private sector—and I do enthusiastically represent the private sector here—similarly needs to go on record admitting that the old free-market paradigm will not forever create enough good jobs to fuel the broad prosperity Americans have come to expect. On our current path the workforce one day will necessarily be *much* larger than work opportunities—even after education reform ensures that as many Americans as possible are educated, and continuously trained, for the high-tech labor market.

So, ladies and gentlemen, you can't put this core problem on hold. We stand at the doorstep of a very interesting, historic, dangerous situation. Risk-taking entrepreneurs will continue to create new wealth as always. But any enterprise must be competitive, or it will die. Uncompetitive ventures create no new wealth, yielding a loss for the risk-taker and a zero for everyone else. Any business must and will adopt 21st Century technological efficiencies to remain competitive, thus narrowing the spigot through which new wealth is broadly shared—job creation.

In other words, ladies and gentlemen, get ready for a hellacious ideological brawl. There will be hand-to-hand combat among those who step up to address this commission. Expect to see blood on this podium while three loud and politically passionate factions battle for your attention.

One faction will be giving you the old "If it ain't broke, don't fix it" routine. Well, it's broke—or soon will be broke. We all know that, or should know that. I suspect even most of the people who will tell you it isn't broke know that it's broke. They're either indulging in wishful thinking, or afraid that admitting the truth will give the bad guys—the ones who will argue with you about where new wealth comes from—an opportunity to win this battle. Pay no attention to either crowd—not the "It ain't broke" crowd, and not the sworn enemies of private-sector prosperity.

That second faction will step up here guns blazing with ideological hollow points. They will cite shrinking working-class and middle-class payrolls, and they will tell you American capitalism has outlived its usefulness. They won't say, "We need to try socialism, we need to give the state a heavier hand on our economic rudder"—because that has always been a tough sell (overtly, at least) to citizens of the world's most successful capitalist nation. But these guys will have gained traction—more traction the longer we delay facing this challenge—because so many Americans are hurting. Keep in mind, ladies and gentlemen, that you just now were video-recorded reaffirming the absolute truth that all new wealth emanates from risk-takers deploying capital in free markets. So ask the crypto-socialists who beg for your ear that same question I always have asked them: "You are very good at distributing wealth. But when the wealth is all gone, what are you going to distribute?"

I hope the third faction will be much larger and louder in this forum than the other two combined. I am, of course, a member of that faction. We say, quite simply, "It *is* broke. Do fix it. But *don't* do anything that will impede risk-takers from creating new wealth." Choking the entrepreneurs would be fatal for us all, including those Americans who are hurting. But we also say, "Don't allow the old capitalist paradigm to slog along until most Americans must depend on some kind of federal soup kitchen for sustenance." That would be just as wrong, just as fatal. We need to find ways to reinforce, restructure, or reinvent the old win-win-win paradigm. We need once again to have business and industry doing well while doing good—creating new wealth, which creates new jobs, which create new wealth, which . . ." We have a sick golden goose. Don't kill it. And don't ignore the illness. Get that precious poultry to the emergency room.

You will not be surprised to learn I have a few ideas—or one big radical idea, if examined under a certain light—about a course of treatment that might help redirect the United States toward its excellent "normal" economic health. I've used up my time, however, and you will be hearing from hundreds of witnesses, most far more eminent thinkers than myself. They will have countless good ideas, and no doubt a few truly terrible ideas. We need lots of good ideas. Just remember this as you analyze them. *It's the technology*. And technology is what it is, no more and no less. No one, most especially an army of bureaucrats, can put technology back in the bottle. It is *irreversible*. We must welcome its positives, adapt to its negatives, and live and prosper in its presence.

I have submitted a few written ideas which I hope you will discuss, consider, and incorporate into your report in some fashion. You have everyone's best wishes, which you'll need.

My imaginary extemporaneous remarks were not, I con-
fess, one-tenth as eloquent as the previous imaginary speaker.
But I stand by the above as a common-sense summary of why
any policy adviser or policymaker should keep the Hippo-
cratic Oath in mind while performing surgery on the world's
greatest economy.

I admit to being not only simplistic but totally vague about
this "commission," or "national convention," or "presidential-
congressional joint advisory group"—or however such a
group might be tasked and organized. The important point I
seek to make is that we need some such body to be impaneled,
with a structure and membership and diverse endorsement
that will make the public, our lawmakers, and our president
pay genuine attention. Deliberations should be televised by
broadcast networks whose executives understand the import
of it all. To that end, the presidents of our top 20 universities,
along with leading academics from every discipline (but especially business, history, and engineering), should issue a joint
call for chartering the new body. If these academics agree that
this could be the most important task-dedicated panel since
the Constitutional Convention, then the academics' joint call
to action should say so. That'll attract some attention.

Done right, with serious intent, the process will launch a
landslide of *global* interest and dialogue. If the world's leading economy and leading manufacturer publicly seeks solutions to the *world's* greatest socioeconomic challenge, then
one imagines that even daytime talk shows might need to
share at least a little of the spotlight. Whether TV programming devoted to the onrushing TECHNOLOGY IMPERATIVE and
the disappearance of American prosperity could outdraw, say,
an Imax movie about an onrushing meteor is, I suppose, less
likely. But we should give it a try.

This national task force might even give our elected political leaders a way to escape now-longstanding abysmal approval ratings. That would only happen, of course, if lawmakers and the administration listened to what the expert panel had to say. Which is still another reason to give these super-advisers—an entire congress of *czars*, we might call them—all the visibility and credibility that can be mustered on their behalf.

While I am intentionally vague in specifications for this extraordinarily important body, whoever formats the panel and appoints its members—the administration, the Congress, the university community—should tell the panelists not to be vague in their deliberations and their report.

Some person or persons of stature—to be forever *at least* as memorable, one hopes, as members of the Watergate Commission or the Warren Commission—will find a phrase of parallel indelibility to Howard Baker's constantly asked question: "What did the president know, and when did he know it?" The new phrase will find a concise way to ask every witness: "If entrepreneurs are not free to create capital, is there any chance this country will not go in the tank? And since we already know the answer to that one, how do we sustain a climate in which entrepreneurs will risk capital and create new wealth *and will share that wealth the way job-creation did in the past?*" That, after all, is what this crisis is all about.

When the panel issues its report it should stand tall and do everything possible to make sure it has not merely generated verbiage for storage. Jointly, credibly, forcefully the panel needs to say what will happen if our little problem with 21st Century technology is defined incorrectly, if the risk-takers are blamed. Then it needs to bring forth solid, innovative ideas for rejuvenating a wounded free-market capitalist system to the benefit of *all*. Does that sound like I am stacking the membership? You tell me. I fully realize many politicians and a few academics believe wealth can be created by legislation or bureaucratic decree or simply by bouncing checks. I don't believe any honestly impaneled body—and certainly none that solves our problem—would lean in that direction.

CHAPTER TEN

Instead of soaking the rich, create some riches

Imagine a social event in which the cocktail hour races off into a sort of rhetorical overdrive. Each conversational cluster splits 50/50 on nearly every topic. Guests circle the room, beverages in hand and politics in mind. Every chat group becomes an ideological scrum. Half the room chants: "Wealthy people rake in an obscene percentage of this country's personal income! Call in the IRS! Soak 'em!" The other half chants: "Are you crazy? This is America! If you make it, you shouldn't have to give it up! Otherwise, why bother achieving success?"

That imaginary back-and-forth can be heard in the real world every day, from co-workers sharing lunch to bellowing broadcasters with listeners coast to coast. Interesting as the debate may be, it is irrelevant because it is the *wrong* debate. What matters most is not how we should define the word "fair." The meaningful question is: Which share-the-wealth mechanism and what formula will yield the best outcome for *all* of us, now and as far into the future as the mind's-eye can see.

The fairness debate does interest me a great deal but it also frustrates me. When a demagogue gets into a strident harangue about "the One Percent" it *angers* me. Not because I have quite a different idea about what is fair (I do), but because unchecked demagoguery on this subject will, in my opinion, destroy our economy on its way to destroying our society. If my opinion is correct we are in very deep trouble, because demagoguery about "the One Percent" is an extremely popular commodity these days.

Let me share a plan—or rather an idea, the outline of a plan—I believe would leap beyond the fairness debate, a scrum on which neither side will win many converts anytime soon. I think such a plan if set in motion would reinforce—to everyone's satisfaction—some basic truths about the source of our nation's wealth. It would do so quickly. It would not be a mere demonstration program. It would create new wealth. It would directly address the perceived "One Percent problem" and would be widely viewed as… *fair*. I believe a strong majority of Americans would support this plan. And just one year following the first April 15 after the plan became law, I think public approval would be even stronger.

But that is only my opinion, and this plan exists—so far as I am aware—only on my own workbench. Call it a Beta version in progress. Think it through as you read this chapter. Ponder its fundamentals. By all means fill in some blanks (there are *many* blanks), look for improvements. In a perfect world any national task force on THE TECHNOLOGY IMPERATIVE (see Chapter Nine) would, among its other chores, assign a committee not to find the best way to "soak the rich," but let's say, more productively, "*optimize what the rich do to grow the economy on behalf of the entire citizenry.*" That seems to me to be infinitely a better idea than "*optimizing the amount of money the rich send to Washington, where much of it will wind up in a monetary landfill.*" My task in this chapter is to lay out this idea/concept/plan compellingly enough that you understand why I think it would succeed, and you can tinker with it on your own workbench. But before we take my prototype for the most meager test flight, Wright Brothers style, let me show you how and why it took shape as it did.

You might interrupt immediately with a question something like: "It sounds to me like you are about to describe some kind of tax plan, otherwise you would not be talking about the 'One Percent problem.' What does that have to do with confronting THE TECHNOLOGY IMPERATIVE?" That's not a digression; it's a very perceptive question. My answer to the tax-plan question is "yes and no." My answer to THE TECHNOLOGY IMPERATIVE question is that this plan goes straight to the heart of the demagoguery that deflects attention from the root cause of our 21st Century challenge. So that's a good place to begin explaining myself.

Every page of this book derives from our country's unwillingness to face up to one core fact. That is, technology plays such a massive role in job loss that one need look no further to find the cause of sustained, long-term—*structural*—unemployment. Even globalization, long cast as the villain in our unemployment drama, is a creature of technological progress. Lately the political rhetoric has focused more on wealthy Americans, with the very highest earners being the most popular target. In some cases, the rhetoric reaches so far past "fairness" issues as to suggest the One Percent somehow got wealthy by stealing millions of jobs and pocketing the vanished paychecks. That is a ridiculous way of skirting THE TECHNOLOGY IMPERATIVE, but the plan outlined here addresses both that phantom complaint and the real reason so many jobs have gone, and will go, missing. In fact, this plan addresses three problems at once:

- *Misconceptions about income inequality.* If a large percentage of Americans believe the affluence of a few has somehow *caused* hard times in the bottom half of the income scale, it doesn't matter politically whether that belief is factually accurate. If enough people in a democracy believe the earth is flat, the next flight to London will soon, by voter demand, disappear above the stratosphere and head outward. The perception of guilt, as all crisis managers know, is as powerful as guilt itself. In hard times, a significant number of Americans are going to demand that the affluent write a check. This plan will make that happen. The money will go to work. And, in my opinion, this plan will serve as an enormous and positive teachable moment in how the American economy best serves the entire country.

• *Actual income inequality.* America became the world's most prosperous nation by creating wealth via free markets. It was an endless rollover of capital that moved an average citizen from a log cabin to, by world standards, the lap of luxury. Except during the worldwide Great Depression, throughout the American Century free-market capitalism created jobs as it created growth. You could not have one without the other. That has changed, in ways we have been discussing since Chapter One. Capitalism is not a thing or a place or a bricks-and-mortar institution. It is a concept, and an irreplaceable one. There is no substitute. The TECHNOLOGY IMPERATIVE, however, means the American concept of capitalism is no longer doing a good job of sharing the wealth in *both* ways it knows how—by creating entrepreneurial opportunity and by creating jobs. We need to steer, adapt, and lubricate American capitalism to meet 21st Century technology realities. We need to do so quickly so the public can see capitalism back on the job. Otherwise, the demagogues will have a clear path for herding us all over a cliff.

• *The need for economic growth.* Even if a vibrant economy were a static and zero-sum game (it isn't), it would need to grow merely to match population increase. Then, because of THE TECHNOLOGY IMPERATIVE, it would have to grow more—a lot more—merely to compensate for jobs that are being replaced by new technology and new efficiencies...a dynamic magnified by global competition. So the famous "bigger pie" must be super-sized just to produce the same sized slices it is feeding us today. We know from historical experiments in communism and socialism that government cannot simply decree all pie slices to be equal. Some will, as Orwell noted, be more equal than others. Worse, the equal-sized slices will begin shrinking immediately because the private sector, deprived of economic freedom and incentive, will not and cannot create statistically significant new wealth. The plan offered here does not remotely claim to be an over-the-counter solution to our "economic growth problem." I do, however, believe it would accomplish everything the much-maligned One Percent can accomplish in that regard.

We all know that if you confiscated the entire 2011 earnings of the highest earners and sent it to Washington, you would solve almost nothing in Washington. Most of us, I hope, understand furthermore that pulling the One Percent's wealth away from the capitalist funnel that feeds our economy would be worse than solving nothing; it would be a serious problem. This plan would, on the other hand, goad the very top layer of American wealth to do everything in its power to grow the economic pie.

I first thought of the plan applying to any person or entity with taxable income of $1 million a year or more. That was partly because a million dollars is certainly a nice income—but also because it's an easy figure with which to work in sorting out numerical concepts. A $1-million cutoff would apply to an army of CEOs and business owners, but also to several battalions of quarterbacks, pitchers, power forwards, rock guitar players, actors, and media performers or executives. Applying the plan to the entire One Percent would cover any household making roughly $506,000 and up. Maybe the plan could be modified and applied effectively to affluent but somewhat lower pay grades. I don't know. Economists and tax experts and actuaries and mathematicians who are whizzes with algorithms—lots of people need to have a go at fine-tuning and improving what I will call here "Economic Growth Corporations."

If anyone thinks a different name might help sell the concept, that's fine. "Economic growth," though, is precisely what these entities would be about. You could call them "Foundations" or "Endowments," but I prefer a word that conveys grassroots economics at work. These Economic Growth Corporations (EGCs) would not be think tanks, or advisory panels, or bureaucracies whose public benefit can be measured only via the most imaginative statistics. EGCs would be chartered to grow the economy in fact, not in theory and not as mere demonstration projects. Each Economic Growth Corporation—scores of them, or why not hundreds?—would respond independently and forcefully to THE TECHNOLOGY IMPERATIVE. An EGC would be the proactive, hard-working, realistic, productive, private-sector alternative to shouting "Jobs! Jobs! Jobs!" in a crowded room. EGCs would jumpstart our economic engine in ways numerous schemes, from "enterprise zones" to your town's tax-abated industrial park, have never done. I regard this paragraph not to be overstated or self-aggrandizing for two reasons. First, THE TECHNOLOGY IMPERATIVE demands that we don't waste time studying ideas that aspire to accomplish less. Second, I am merely offering a schematic drawing, not detailed blueprints. Poking, prodding, modification, amplification, and improvement are welcomed and expected. Due diligence on all details will be vital.

Chapter Nine's imaginary national convention—or a specially tasked academic task force, or a bipartisan and presidential commission of *private citizens*—would have to pull this plan together in great detail, right down to stating the process for obtaining an Economic Growth Corporation charter, qualifications for board membership, and so on. Perhaps Congress could lend staff support to the convention/commission's work. Or perhaps business and industry and leading foundations (somebody write a grant!) could fund the sessions. Enabling legislation would need to be drafted, approved by 435 members of the House, 100 members of the Senate, and signed by one guy at the White House. They could then turn the ceremonial first shovel of dirt, get out of the way, and watch the results. The idea as it leaves my desk is a private-sector plan. Intensely so. I can't see it being successful any other way.

Not long before this book went to press I shared lunch with a very close friend whose ideas tend to land just left of center. This means, essentially, that he possesses more faith in non-essential government endeavors than I do. We discuss conflicting views with the kind of collegial civility that unfortunately has disappeared from most public discourse. I told him about my idea, in which government is involved only to enable the plan and share its rewards. I fielded questions while he did his own poking and prodding. My friend knows that not only do I believe private equity capitalism serves the American economy very well, but that I *was* a practicing private equity capitalist. After conversational due diligence he pronounced Economic Growth Corporations to be a most interesting idea, and perhaps—after further study—a worthy one.

Why? Because, he said, it isn't "just more private equity capital theory." I of course would say a major reason EGCs will work is that they aren't "just another zero-sum government bureaucracy that can spend wealth but can't create wealth."

A collegial lunch conversation does not guarantee consensus for a major national initiative. On the other hand, it has been so long since this country achieved consensus on important issues that any hint of a shared vision is encouraging. In government, the once meaningful word "bipartisan" has been replaced by "dead on arrival." Media consumers surf toward the comfort of their own special interests. Different generations haven't sat in the same room together, figuratively and generally speaking, since Ed Sullivan went off the air and took puppet acts, the Metropolitan Opera, and the Beatles with him. Maybe a campaign to create and implement an EGC network can pull a strong majority of us, in direct response to THE TECHNOLOGY IMPERATIVE at least, onto the same page. Some Americans feel as much need to be protected from capitalists as I feel need to be protected from bureaucrats and politicians run amok. Thinking of the EGC plan in the same breath with what Congress and the President did in the case of the Simpson-Bowles commission on national debt only makes me feel that need all the more. On this paramount issue, socioeconomic survival in the 21st Century, I believe free markets have *everything* to do with success. I believe a rejuvenated American capitalism comprises our *only* way forward. Surely we can somehow steer the birthing of Economic Growth Corporations away from the political morass? I hope so.

Our best ideas usually emanate from both the random insights of experience and the disciplined input of directed thought. Ideas percolate subconsciously until appearing in one's mind not quite in focus and with some assembly required. Or I should say that's the way it works for me. All the bases an idea touches in the birthing process can be important to understanding, evaluating, and improving an idea, especially a big idea. I could claim I had an epiphany about "economic growth corporations"—that after living the entrepreneurial life, devoting countless thousands of hours to thinking about "pragmatic economics," enjoying rewarding relationships with academics and executives on several continents, blogging, writing management textbooks, teaching related university courses, and pondering THE TECHNOLOGY IMPERATIVE for most of a lifetime…I *suddenly had this vision*. Not likely.

In truth this idea, new as it is (to my knowledge it's unique), feels more like a plan someone of my background might have been *destined* to develop in a lively and vital debate about how to solve a well-defined problem. If one understands that new technology is not only the world's most powerful force for sweeping change but is totally apolitical, and if one understands that government can print money but can't create wealth, then it's almost as if sooner or later one will write this book and in the process think of something very similar to Economic Growth Corporations. So before our little test flight, let's run down a brief checklist. These are stipulations, compelling facts, and informed (and widely held) opinions that no doubt helped generate, both intuitively and logically, my answer to the question: "If government can't do what's needed and never could, and if the private sector suddenly isn't doing it very well, and if the public dialogue has some wild idea that confiscating wealth from the rich will solve the problem…then what should we do?" Several items are shorthand for topics already discussed; others are new to our discussion, and are fleshed out a bit:

- The United States has flourished because of its capitalist economy. Free market entrepreneurialism creates new wealth, which is the only way to grow a nation's economic pie, which is the only way to sustain and share prosperity.
- Technological progress has achieved a critical mass in which the economy can grow and create new wealth without creating enough new jobs.
- This untenable situation has sparked a misguided populism in which Americans whose fortunes are in decline, and politicians who see a floodtide rushing toward the voting booth, seek—in the name of "fairness"—to confiscate wealth and share it.
- That said, we absolutely *do* have a social (compared with a merely political) need to distribute newly created wealth more broadly—just as American capitalism did through most of the 20th Century.
- For America to prosper, wealth—capital—must constantly move along a productive channel. Money must be invested in new businesses, new product lines, new technology, new services. This is truer than ever, because an ever larger economy is required to keep up with population growth and THE TECHNOLOGY IMPERATIVE.
- When risk-takers are successful, it creates new wealth for them and—via wages and salaries—for whatever number of new employees technology decrees to be competitive. Those new employees then go out and move that money again as consumers. The risk-takers are also, of course, consumers—and continue investing, thus creating more new wealth. Wealth distribution on the old model has been a wondrous, sustainable thing that makes this country's wheels go around. For sure, let's *invest* some wealth to get the wheels turning again. We *must* do so. But we cannot *confiscate* wealth. We

cannot simply find the largest bank accounts and order them shared. But neither can we let anyone remove a huge pile of money from the economy and use it as a place to sit.

• Serious attempts to quantify "government waste" (the 1980s Grace Commission, for example) have estimated that as much as one-third of federal revenue disappears into a monetary landfill. Three decades after the Grace Commission a gaggle of federal bureaucrats still managed to spend $823,000 entertaining themselves during a trip to Las Vegas. Do you think confiscating wealth from those who pay $823,000 a year to the IRS will solve any unemployment problems? Do you think the United States, during what could be called "the government era," has some miles to travel before anyone with that kind of tax liability will be—as the immigrants used to say—"proud to pay his taxes?" How would you like to write an $823,000 check to the IRS and discover you didn't even buy one spaghetti lunch for an Appalachian eighth-grader, but you did pay to hire a Las Vegas magician to entertain bureaucrats at poolside? Even as we discuss a 21st Century crisis caused by private-sector *efficiency*, it is *inefficiency* and dysfunctional management that best characterize government. An astonishing percentage of federal revenue is spent, for example, merely to service our mounting national debt. The big-three entitlement programs teeter on the edge of bankruptcy by any sane accounting principle. The federal government is not a place to send capital for safekeeping, let alone growth; it has become a place where resources shrink and debt grows.

• Entering "U.S. Tax Code" into the Amazon.com books search engine recently yielded 1,254 hits. "U.S. Tax Code" returned 299,000,000 hits on a Google search—nearly one hit for every American man, woman, and child. General Electric earned $14 billion in 2010, paid no federal income tax, but sent the IRS a 57,000-page return (thankfully, an electronic return) that was more than 10,000 pages *shorter* than the Tax Code itself. The Tax Code in my opinion has done more damage to American business than anything else on a long list of factors requiring damage control. Our tax law does this even as it generates sound bites and headlines—such as "No Tax Bill for GE"—that are red meat for political demagogues. The Tax Code is a nightmare for business even though countless thousands of pages entered the Tax Code because of lobbying on behalf of one industry or another. The Tax Code is a hopelessly unfathomable, inefficient, counter-productive constraint on the American economy no matter who might be responsible for any particular exemption or billion-dollar footnote, many of which exist only to squelch competition. I said it is impossible these days to find consensus on any major issue. I forgot for a moment that Republicans, Democrats, righties, lefties, country bumpkins, city slickers—*everyone* agrees the Tax Code needs to be chopped, simplified...probably ripped up entirely and rewritten.

• If we want to adapt our capitalist economy so it works amid 21st Century realities, and if we are thinking of something toward the kind of entity I have been describing, then it must be something transparent but non-governmental. It needs to be a forceful presence in the economy. It needs to keep capital moving and creating wealth. It needs to be run by people whose education and experience and talents are from and of that process—private sector managers and engineers and successful entrepreneurs who, for example, will exercise fundamental due diligence and not funnel capital toward a Solyndra debacle.

After reading the above checklist of thought-process influences, some readers will believe my idea springs from an anti-government mindset, someone who lacks understanding and vision when it comes to citizens who find themselves unable, despite their best efforts, to earn a living wage. Quite the opposite.

I would laugh at the suggestion that I am an anti-government type if it did not illustrate how far America's definition of "government" has swung toward statism. Before emigrating to America I lived in a poor neighborhood that had been emptied and then resettled during a forced population exchange involving millions of Greeks and Turks. I lived in that neighborhood when the Nazi paratroopers invaded and occupied Crete. I lived there during the civil war that followed. My childhood, adolescence, studies, and world travels have given me an excellent idea of what instability, and even anarchy, are all about. Anyone who knows these things has profound respect for government's role in civilized society. America's constitutional democratic republic *is* deservedly a model for the world. This doesn't mean I can't be an avid proponent of, as they used to say, "good government." The world's best political system gives us government that is only as good as current and recent officeholders, voters, bureaucrats, and the forces of inertia might provide. Too much government doesn't work any better for the majority of citizens than too little government. Good government, in other words, is a work in eternal progress.

Regarding my understanding and vision about the economic plight of ordinary people, anyone who has thought seriously about THE TECHNOLOGY IMPERATIVE understands that millions of Americans have been rejected by the traditional workplace. Ultimately even the new workplace will need fewer and fewer employees, even tech-qualified employees.

Long-term, we will need to reinvent the word "job." Finding new ways for people to live creative, productive lives with dignity has been, therefore, very much on my mind. But first we need to re-engage a robustly growing economy under circumstances of *this* moment. That's where the idea of Economic Growth Corporations enters into the picture—riding aboard, of all vehicles, the United States Tax Code.

It is instructive that almost anything one might say to illustrate the Tax Code's negative impact on our economy is (a) well-known, and (b) ignored by Congress. For instance, the Great Recession of 2008 made any American who follows the news—even someone who avoids business news whenever possible—aware of two key concepts that impede creation of new wealth inside the United States, which is where we want to see new wealth created. The first concept refers to "money sitting on the sidelines," meaning money that is not productively *in motion*—not being invested as capital, not even put in circulation to buy things. (Don't forget, if some tycoon buys a multi-million-dollar yacht, that purchase means millions of dollars going into the pockets of shipyard employees.) The second concept refers to American corporations holding many billions of dollars in foreign earnings offshore, where all that idle cash does absolutely nothing to create American jobs. Put just these two sources of idle dollars into motion inside the United States and you will have a huge stimulus package involving neither a penny of your tax bill nor an ounce of involvement by the federal bureaucracy. It is more complex than that. Tax attorneys and congressional staffers and the IRS do find things to do with their time.

Idle money, however, *is* idle. It is no more productive than a road worker leaning on his shovel. Less productive, actually, because the road worker will soon be out spending his paycheck. Money can "go to the sidelines" for lots of reasons, but often enough the reason is tax law (using money to create wealth can be a very punitive activity depending which clause of the Tax Code applies, and when). As for "repatriating capital," U.S. corporations can be taxed up to 35 percent *on foreign earnings they bring home*, so companies leave the cash there or invest it there or do a Tax Code waltz in which they spend *years* bringing the earnings home. (Does General Electric's 2010 tax return begin to make more sense?)

These images of idle money are murkier than swamp water because of varying tax rates and exemptions and deductions, special levies, etc. I am not a tax attorney and can't go into detail, for which you should be grateful. That is the very point made in the futile cries of Tax Code critics. "Simplify it! Toss out nonsensical tax breaks! Level the playing field!" Absolutely. Let's do it. Then let's see how much capital is in motion, how much is on the sidelines, and how much is sitting on the dock in some other country. Let's say the situation is much improved (it will be). No matter—Economic Growth Corporations are an idea that will *still* optimize movement of capital, stimulate business activity in all 50 states, and create wealth. The actuaries and the Congressional Budget Office and the economics professors can all estimate the dollar impact and the job-creation impact far better than I. But it is guaranteed to happen.

Here's how and why.

Our hypothetical target here is a man named, of course, Taxpayer Jones. He has had a very good year. His taxable income is $1 million. His tax rate is 15 percent. I am pulling that rate from thin air. I lean toward preference for a sort of flat-tax scheme, but that doesn't matter. Jones's tax rate could be higher or lower, and could result from a 300-page return under the current Tax Code or a postcard-sized return under some future legislation. What matters is that for purposes of illustration Taxpayer Jones is in a 15 percent bracket, he made a million bucks, and on April 15th he owes $150,000 to the IRS. Here, on the other hand, is what would happen if Economic Growth Corporations were operating across the United States.

Mr. Jones has a choice. He can invest up to half of his $1-million taxable income in Economic Growth Corporation stock. This could be one investment in one EGC or any number of EGCs—one in his hometown, for example, that invests only in regional startup companies. Or one back East that invests there. Or one in Chicago that invests in energy developers from coast to coast. (All EGCs, by the way, would be required to make 100 percent of their investments in enterprises operating on U.S. soil.) Mr. Jones has no specific control over how his money will be invested. He will, like any other American, be able to click online to see who sits on an EGC's board, what their current portfolio looks like, and view a prospectus outlining their investment philosophy. Other than that, Mr. Jones is buying into, essentially, a blind trust—one that, incidentally, is operated exactly like a world-class private equity fund. That is, in fact, one reason Taxpayer Jones will choose to send his money in that direction. That is the carrot.

The other reason—the substantial stick—kicks in if Taxpayer Jones decides he'd rather not invest half his after-tax (15 percent tax) income in an Economic Growth Corporation, would rather not use the EGC statute to boost the economy, would rather not create new wealth and new jobs this way, would rather not do all the good things that happen when money goes out and gets to work. In that case, the tax rate on half of his income will double, from 15 percent to 30 percent. He can use what's left to buy a boat, or invest elsewhere, or stick in a mattress…whatever he likes. But instead of writing the IRS a $150,000 check on his $1 million, he will write a check for $225,000…15 percent on the first $500,000 earned, 30 percent on the second $500,000. If he wishes to invest, say, $200,000 in EGC stock, he will pay 15 percent tax on $700,000 income and 30 percent on $300,000, and so on.

The very first thing I need to remind you of is that these tax rates are *hypothetical*, though the generality—doubling the rate on the second half of income strikes me as about right. The main idea is to make the penalty for non-investment high enough to encourage it, but not so high as to encourage non-activity on Mr. Jones's part (as in not earning the money in the first place) or hiding income, legally or illegally, as the Tax Code monstrosity and all those tax lawyers currently enable.

Each Economic Growth Corporation would be required to meet stringent yardsticks for board experience and talent and expertise…to avoid conflicts of interest in all obvious respects…and to maintain the highest standards of board oversight and managerial due diligence. Each EGC's board would include men and women with a broad range of both financial and managerial background. As individuals and collectively they will know how to assess the present and future worth of an existing company, or a nascent company, or a product, or a process, or an idea. They will invest accordingly, unimpeded by bureaucratic regulations beyond what you see here and the usual statutes governing equity trading. And, of course, the requirement that all investments go to enterprises on U.S. soil.

Like a private equity firm, the EGC would seek out investment opportunities in the form of either start-ups or enhanced operations for existing firms—or the outright purchase of an existing firm that melds well into the EGC portfolio. That portfolio will grow, winning some and losing some, but winning more than losing and in any case operating with Taxpayer Jones's money—not yours—and putting 100 percent of that money out into the economy rather than into Washington, Inc. Because of their independence, all EGCs will be in efficient competition to find winning startup ideas and productive innovations for existing companies. Putting their investment capital to work in that direction will achieve what we all want them to achieve, just as it says on their shingles—*economic growth*. A million dollars invested by an EGC—let's say Midwest Construction Partnerships, EGC—will create jobs. Guaranteed, as I said. That is more than one can say for an endless string of situations where government tried to be a player and instead wound up being played.

An Economic Growth Corporation would have the same beginnings and endings as a private equity firm. The EGC would be chartered, organized, capital raised for a set period of time (often seven years), and the new entity would be put to work creating wealth. When the EGC's expiration date arrives, it can sell itself to another EGC, can sell stock back to companies it has invested in, or it can go public and move from EGC status to a stock exchange listing under a new name—or simply with that "EGC" dropped from business cards. All those disbursement options produce a cash return. That cash goes back to Taxpayer Jones and his fellow investors. If it is a profitable investment, Mr. Jones has income to be taxed on *that* year's IRS return. Let's give the imaginary Technology Imperative convention's special committee on EGCs the task of ironing out details of carry-forwards for losses and such.

I could spend many pages just skimming the possible elements and variations of this schematic plan. What if, to cite just one example, we are talking about someone who is really, really, really rich? Or just really rich? Should there be a sliding scale of penalties—an opportunity, in other words, to get a bigger reward for EGC investing (and a bigger penalty for not investing) depending on how much stratospheric income one has available to invest? Should the middle class—if someone in the middle class has done enough financial planning to be able to send half his income away for seven years—be allowed to participate? If so, how will rewards and penalties be structured? Who pays to buy office furniture and turn on the lights as an EGC is being formed? Should there be a clearinghouse helping prospective EGCs (or communities that wish to charter an EGC) choose directors and get started? Endless possibilities, endless *necessities*.

It is the framework that matters here. It makes sense to me. It would have made a lot of sense 50 years ago. In the face of THE TECHNOLOGY IMPERATIVE, I believe it makes many times more sense than it did then.

EGCs will work better if the U.S. Tax Code is scrapped and replaced with a simple set of personal and corporate brackets. EGCs will work better if government regulatory bureaucracies do far less to discourage business activity (but that is a topic for a book nearly as thick as the Tax Code). Economic Growth Corporations would work better if our educational system were better prepared for the 21st Century. EGCs would work better if our public infrastructure were not so decrepit, and if the manufacturing infrastructure were 100 percent world-class. A beauty part of this plan is that it will make things happen before, during, and after all these optimizing factors have been achieved. You will believe that to be true if you envision, as I do, an absolute certainty that EGCs will put capital into the marketplace, stir business activity, move money, create wealth. I do also believe that the EGC concept dovetails nicely with desperately needed Tax Code reform, and would have an impact on tax avoidance (not evasion, avoidance).

As important as the risk-takers are, I am not anointing entrepreneurs as the heroes of this or any similar plan. Free-market risk-takers do not charge into a suicide mission. But neither do they, when invited to create new wealth, demand a sure thing. What they require is a risk that will, if successful, produce an appropriate reward. Doing well by doing good is not merely a clever, if clichéd, phrase; it is the American way. The gentlemen farmers who founded this nation did not intend Mt. Vernon or Monticello to be non-profits. When Economic Growth Corporations begin pulling money off the sidelines and into the wealth-creating fray, the personal and corporate risk-takers who send their dollars for investment will deserve credit for being successful business men and women—no more, no less. EGCs will give risk-takers incentive for trying to do well by putting their wealth to work. The hero of the tale will be a rejuvenated free market itself. Priming that pump will generate—along with smart policymaking—enough of a surge, one hopes, to give us time and resources for education reform, infrastructure upgrades, and for planning the heavy lifting that lies ahead as THE TECHNOLOGY IMPERATIVE exerts more and more influence on society.

Economic Growth Corporations, as outlined here, will beyond *any* doubt lure capital from top earners. "Top earners" includes individuals and corporations and single proprietor businesses—any entity filing with the IRS. But just as the experts might wish to extend EGC eligibility down to lower income levels, perhaps non-profits (foundations, principally) and non-individual entities (insurance portfolios, pension funds, trusts) regardless of balance sheets should be penciled into the plan in some way with differing incentives. The idea, after all, is to find capital, wherever it might be holed up, and channel it into a flood of new investment. For those with tax liabilities, all that's required is to adapt and reduce thousands and thousands of Tax Code pages to a simple two-sentence concept: "If you help keep money moving directly into this great economic engine of ours, we will reward you. If you decide to use or spend that same money in any other way, we will punish you."

If this plan were to be refined and passed into law, I think it would a good thing to have all 535 lawmakers plus the president and vice-president be present for the first EGC christening. Just a reminder to *everyone* about where our prosperity comes from.

What hath technology wrought?

On May 24, 1844, the painter and inventor Samuel F.B. Morse took center stage among a group gathered in the U.S. Supreme Court chambers, housed at that time in the Capitol basement. Morse was demonstrating his electromagnetic telegraph to mark the official launch of a pathfinding service that reached 30 miles, from Washington to Baltimore. He clicked out dots and dashes to spell a Bible quote chosen by the daughter of the U.S. patent commissioner: "What hath God wrought." Sending and receiving a telegram required a code-skilled operator, who could transmit 30 characters per minute. Another operator on the other end was needed to translate the code, and unless the recipient came to the Baltimore train station a courier would be needed to hand deliver the message. Thirty-two years later Alexander Graham Bell shouted into a mouthpiece: "Mr. Watson, come here—I want to see you." It was an iconic moment that yielded another of history's most famous quotes. The world press corps, on the other hand, paid no attention to whatever was said by the first shopper who prowled grocery aisles while conversing, by cell phone, with someone on the other side of the earth. Such is technological progress. Such are ever-higher expectations for the next gizmo. Such is the easy danger of not paying enough attention to how new technology impacts society.

Technology's great, obvious impact has been upon life's

most precious commodity, time. Only a few generations ago our ancestors worked long hours, six days a week, often in dangerous settings. Most, whether working a dangerous job or not, did not live long enough or well enough to enjoy retirement. Today's exploding entertainment and sports industries, plugged-in internet lifestyle, and freedom for both household partners to get out and enter the workforce all derive from "spare" time provided by technology. How ironic that as technology delivers more and more hours and days for us to use as we wish, technology also is about to deliver the greatest socioeconomic conundrum of the century. Citizens of the developed world will have too much spare time and not enough hours on the job. Society will need to adapt. Eventually we will need to reinvent our relationship with the workplace— wherever and whatever the workplace might be.

This is not science fiction. It is our genuine challenge. The transition's fully realized phase—when traditional "unemployment" reaches such a large, sustained number as to make the word meaningless—lies somewhere over the horizon. We have no real idea how far into the future, anymore than Samuel F.B. Morse knew that three decades after he set wires to clicking, Alexander Graham Bell would set wires to talking. The leap from Bell to the internet took more than another century. Predicting the arrival date of massive technological impact is futile, but predicting its certainty is easy. This time-shifting upheaval *will* happen. It already has begun, even if many have chosen to label the cause as "globalization" or ignore it altogether behind the blinders of ideology and politics. Fact is, we live today on the leading edge of THE TECHNOLOGICAL IMPERATIVE.

When facing such a visionary challenge (meaning its most powerful consequences won't happen tomorrow or the next day), it is tempting to set the proactive response aside in favor of the spectator approach. What we are facing, after all, is one of those *irreversible* consequences of technological progress. The challenge, however, is not to reverse the irreversible, but, as always, to find the best path toward coexisting with, and even flourishing amid, a new era's reality. The positive here is familiar and obvious—still more "spare" time, though even I do not foresee technology adding a 25th hour to humanity's days. The negatives (or the challenges, I prefer to say) are huge, spanning the spectrum of socioeconomic wants and needs and the structure of society itself. Clearly, the way most of us "make a living" will need redefining. Clearly, quality of life will become a dominant issue in the opposite of the way it was for, say, a coal miner who rarely saw daylight and was too tired to enjoy it when he did. Clearly, proponents of Big Brother statism in one form or another will seek to win out in competition for hearts and minds as society seeks to find its best way to cope, organically, with a new world that even Columbus could not have imagined.

I see no way the statists, the socialists, or even more benign big-government advocates can do right by the American people. In other words, I see no zero-sum system ever serving as an acceptable substitute for creating wealth within a free-market system—not even in a futuristic, strange new world where capitalism loses most of its *traditional* means of sharing share the wealth by creating jobs. Meanwhile, I readily concede that will be a moot point unless American free-market capitalism repairs itself during the transition from now to then. My suggested Economic Growth Corporations are one example meant to be implemented almost instantaneously, a very specific idea but one whose root—getting the capitalist system back to creating and sharing wealth before it is too

late—will apply to every phase of THE TECHNOLOGY IMPERA-
TIVE. We must achieve that, or some version of a Big Brother
society will be inevitable.

Every human, I believe, is meant to aspire and, through the
mechanism of competitive *opportunity*, to achieve everything
he or she is capable of achieving. A statist society in which
people are incentivized to rely on handouts at worst or bloated
bureaucratic employment at best, rather than relying on their
own realistic aspirations and training and labor and creativity,
is doomed to fail. Such societies are the antithesis of what the
American founders had in mind. True, the founders would
no doubt be mystified and mortified if they were to assemble
next week and forced to ponder THE TECHNOLOGY IMPERATIVE.
I believe, however, the same free-market spirit the founders
evoked in the 18th Century would be rewritten into their ideas
for the 21st Century. I think almost everyone can agree with
that assertion. The trick is how to flesh out those ideas and
how to get them realized, and that is why we need a national
dialogue on these things now, rather than taking a spectator-
to-history approach. We know where the passive, spectator
approach will end up.

I will not draw even one schematic, as I did with the EGC
concept, to suggest ways of resuscitating and sustaining our
free-market economic engine as technology decimates the
need for human labor, then decimates it again, and again, and
then again. I do challenge all capitalist practitioners and free-
market advocates, though, to acknowledge and respond to
THE TECHNOLOGY IMPERATIVE. Technology is trying to make
you obsolete. You *will* be obsolete—or rather, you *will* be dis-
carded—if our free-market system does not adapt to today's
challenges, let alone the upheaval that lies ahead. For today,
we need to optimize the job-creation part of the mechanism.

In the futuristic part of the equation, we cannot rely on Henry Ford and other pathfinders to create a brand-new employment paradigm. We know free markets will, if allowed, continue to create new wealth even as job creation slows. But we need to be looking for new ways our capitalist system can broadly distribute the wealth it creates. If we don't, there will be just two possible outcomes: a government-dominated economy and society, or a revolution—not in the figurative but the literal sense.

The private sector must, at every step of our social and technological evolution, provide our citizens the ability and the incentive to seek and sustain a rewarding, productive life. The middleman in Washington, D.C., cannot do that. Our government can protect us from those who would do us harm, can pursue vital public-works projects that the private sector cannot accomplish, and can in fact rightfully pursue any necessary endeavor the private sector cannot do better and more efficiently. Few such endeavors exist.

One thing the public sector most definitely can*not* do is create prosperity. This little book has been deservedly tough on ideologues who somehow believe otherwise. The private sector, too, has some obligations and limitations in the social contract. In this century, that will mean, above all, honest and effective response to THE TECHNOLOGY IMPERATIVE. The real safety net is not a zero-sum proposition.

I suspect that in the end the best solution will include a large dose of—surprise!—the entrepreneurial spirit, in one form or another. If corporate America, for example, were to sustain some quasi-"foundations," some entities or mechanism, for helping all who are willing and able to operate single-proprietor endeavors—from crafts to artisanal output to musical performance to tutoring to an endless list of service skills—that would be one example of new wealth being created and shared (and then creating more wealth) without intervention or waste or fiscal self-aggrandizement by the federal government. That suggestion is intentionally vaguer than vague. It is the bypassing of Washington and the preserving of the free-market system that I wish to illustrate. That is not a blueprint. It is just a citizen standing at roadside and pointing in the direction of where this pilgrimage needs to be heading.

We need lots of ideas, soon, on how to get there.

ACKNOWLEDGMENTS

This book owes its existence to two quite different causal agents.

The first is my growing frustration and anger (shared by millions of Americans) with our public leadership's inability to grasp our fundamental 21st Century socioeconomic problems and challenges. I am not grateful for that frustration and anger, but it needs acknowledging.

The second is my writing partner and friend, Tom W. Ferguson. In the text I refer to him as "my editor"—which he is, because all the thoughts and suggestions in this book are my own. But to be clear, he has been the one who—as he often says—"pushes words around on the screen." I hope my thoughts are interesting and at times perhaps even useful. If they are also readable, that is Tom's fault.